PSYCHIATRIC MUSIC THERAPY
Origins and Development

Florence Tyson

CREATIVE ARTS REHABILITATION CENTER

Creative Arts Rehabilitation Center
New York

Library of Congress Cataloging in Publication Data
Tyson, Florence.
    Psychiatric music therapy—origins and development.

    Bibliography: p. 73
    includes indexes.
    1. Music therapy. I. Title.   (DNLM: Music therapy. WM 450.5.M8 T 994p)
ML 3920.T95   616.89′1654   81-69631
ISBN 0-9606876-0-2   AACR2
ISBN 0-9606876-1-0 (pbk.)

Fred Weidner & Son Printers, Inc.
New York
Cover Design: Communigraphics, New York

*To the fierce beauty and struggle
of those who have come to
Creative Arts Rehabilitation Center
in search of expressive pathways
toward emotional and social growth
through our beloved arts.*

Table of Contents

Acknowledgements

Some of the material describing the transition of music therapy from a hospital to a community-based practice has appeared previously in the following professional publications:

MUSIC THERAPY 1958 — "The Development of an Out-Patient Music Therapy Referral Service." Allen Press, Lawrence, Kansas, 1959

PSYCHIATRIC QUARTERLY — "Therapeutic Elements in Out-Patient Music Therapy." State Hospitals Press, Utica, N.Y., v. 39, No. 2, April 1965

PSYCHIATRIC QUARTERLY SUPPLEMENT—"Music Therapy Practice in the Community—Three Case Histories." State Hospitals Press, Utica, N.Y., Part I, 1966

MUSIC IN THERAPY, (Ed.) E. Thayer Gaston—"The Community Music Therapy Center." The Macmillan Co., New York, 1968

JOURNAL OF MUSIC THERAPY (with Ludwig, A. J.) — "A Song for Michael—The Use of Music Therapy as an Educational Modality within a Situation of Progressive Organic Deterioration." National Association for Music Therapy, Inc., Lawrence, Kansas, v. VI, No. 3, Fall, 1969

JOURNAL OF MUSIC THERAPY—"Guidelines Toward the Organization of Clinical Music Therapy Programs in the Community." National Association for Music Therapy, Inc., Lawrence, Kansas, v. X, No. 3, Fall, 1973

ART PSYCHOTHERAPY—"Child at the Gate—Individual Music Therapy with a Schizophrenic Woman." Pergamon Press Ltd., Elmsford, N.Y., v. 6, 1979

I am also indebted to Tavistock Publications Ltd., London, England, for permission to quote generously from Michael Balint's BASIC FAULT (1968) in the concluding section "Music and the Primary Relationship."

Preface

The idea for Creative Arts Rehabilitation Center grew out of my experiences supervising and training music therapists in state and city mental hospitals, as Director of the Mental Health Division, Musicians Emergency Fund, Inc., starting in 1952. There was ample opportunity to observe the impact of music therapy upon seriously-ill psychiatric patients, some of whom became amenable to medical treatment and socialization processes for the first time while hospitalized, through their ability to communicate and relate nonverbally in music therapy. Upon discharge, however, the lack of a continuum of similar supportive services in the community inevitably led the patient to deepening isolation and withdrawal, and return to the hospital.

In 1963, a small circle of unusually dedicated staff and friends formed the independent Creative Arts Rehabilitation Center, Inc.; their commitment and support have helped to realize a psychiatric rehabilitation agency in the community whose central program consists of all creative arts therapies—music, dance, art, drama and poetry. Over the years, the circles have widened to include the participation of many more exceptionally devoted colleagues and supporters, which further advanced the continuity and growth of the organization. Space does not permit a listing of their names—I can only express my eternal gratitude to them for their willingness to share the adventure, as well as the risks and sacrifices of an unprecedented situation, without thought of gain for themselves.

In particular, I want to thank Board members Joan Winer Brown for her persuasive encouragement and active efforts in behalf of my writing, and to Mrs. Louis H. Harris and Mr. Leo Model for making possible the publication of this monograph. I am also indebted to Dr. Alice Shields for invaluable technical assistance in the preparation and completion of the manuscript.

F.T.

Introduction

Music is a universal human phenomenon that can, perhaps, best be understood from a holistic viewpoint.

No one of us is a stranger to the effects of music in our daily lives. We have all had the experience of responding in different ways to its different forms — whether they be spirited march, exuberant rhumba, pounding rock and roll, yearning love song, mournful dirge or Bach cantata. Similarly, from time immemorial, human beings have turned to music for its remarkable powers of emotional and spiritual renewal, and of aesthetic fulfillment.

The many facets of music—its capacity to arouse feelings, its associative content based on words or patterns, its sheer sensual beauty, its rhythmic vitality, its technical complexities—are as limitless as man's potentialities to create. Music grew in complexity in response to cultural and social developments; its evolution parallels that of other art forms, which together closely follow the ongoing growth of human knowledge. It is only in recent years that this multi-faceted art is being put to use with awareness, through music therapy, to assist in the rehabilitation of physically and mentally ill people.

> Music presents to the ear an array of auditory patterns which at a purely formal level are very similar, if not identical with, the bodily patterns which are the basis of real emotion. The two kinds of pattern are with respect to their form practically the same, but the auditory pattern makes music whereas the visceral and organic patterns make emotion. Music sounds the way emotions feel (Pratt, 1952).

The roots of the word "emotion" derive from "emovere," meaning *to move out*. Feelings generate an impulse toward open action. Just as among primitive peoples, the rattle was used to render forearm movements audible (Hughes, 1948), so does it seem that music arose as an audible expression of our internal reactions to sensory, motor and psychological stimuli. Such audible correspondences serve to 1) complete or actualize the human organism; 2) reassure the individual by objectifying his presence in the environment; 3) communicate the individual's presence and feeling state to his fellows, and 4) assist as an instrument of bonding the individual with his fellows in groups.

More fundamental even than the relationship to emotion may be the analogy between music and physiological communication. Biological rhythms include a system of neuron impulses which communicates at a

1

pre-conscious level throughout the entire nervous system. Rimland (1964) has called this process "neuron entelechy," from which he builds a genetic explanation of behavior. Before man acquired language, he passed through an intermediate stage of development, in which bodily rhythms began to be imitated in overt behavior. This is considered to be the earliest phase of ego development (Hudson, 1973).

The organic link between music and the human being provides the groundwork from which the music therapy profession evolved. Most of music therapy practice lies in the area of emotional illness, which is characterized by marked withdrawal, inhibition, the repression of denial or feelings, or the dissociation therefrom. It is the task of the music therapist to bring about behavioral change — to induce emotional and social growth—through functional applications of music. As "movement is the source of all change" (Klee, 1958), we can see in the very origins of music the means for addressing the problem. Particularly with psychiatric patients, a primary aim of the music therapy process is to re-activate feelings through musical stimuli and encourage their "outflow" (Tyson, 1965) through expressive or motoric channels. By so doing, the individual is helped to experience, perceive and integrate his/her inner reality, and direct it into greater consonance with needs, desires and goals to be realized in outer reality. The organic interrelationship between man's emotional responses and his physical being suggests why music has been so closely associated with medicine since the beginning of recorded history (Apel, 1969).

Origins of Music
and Medicine

Although the origins of music itself remain obscure, there seems little doubt that they evolved from the sounds and rhythms in nature. Stumph believes they originated in signal calls (Diserens and Fine, 1939); Nadel (1930) ascribes it to the need for a special language with which to communicate with the supernatural; Schneider (1957) emphasizes the importance of the totemistic concept, i.e., the voices of spirits (dead ancestors) dwell in natural objects; by imitating these voices, primitive man sought union with his dead ancestors, who determined the course of the world. Hughes (1948) ascribes the development of musical rhythm to word rhythms and poetry, and to the dance; clapping the hands, stamping the feet, and slapping the thighs or the belly were among the earliest modes of reinforcing dance rhythms, and such manifestations at a remote period led to the invention of primitive instruments of percussion.

Among primitive peoples, illness was seen as arising from magico-religious forces (Sigerist, 1944) or from the breaking of taboos. Music, in combination with dance or words, was used to enhance the magical practices of the priest-practitioner. Songs, as well as the musical instruments which accompanied them — drum, rattle, flute or bells — were considered efficacious in exorcising disease or healing wounds (Radin, 1948).

In classical antiquity, disease was regarded as a disharmony between man's physical and psychical nature. Music was considered a form of divine revelation (Boxberger, 1961), and profoundly important in bringing about harmony, or health. The ancients defined music as the arts of the Muses (from which the word "music" derives), which included poetry, singing, playing and interpretive dancing; harmony, melody and rhythm were their chief constituents (Meinecke, 1948). Among Greek divinities, Apollo, leader of the Muses and god of music, was also regarded as the founder of medicine. His medicative powers represented the healing powers of nature.

Pythagoras, the nature-philosopher (c. 582–c. 500 B.C.), believed that health depended upon an ordered harmony within both mind and body. He expounded a daily regimen of diet and music which would assure "catharsis." It is still astonishing to realize that, through his studies of the physics of sound and of the monochord, he fixed the ratios of the perfect consonant intervals—the octave, fifth and fourth—which are still funda-

3

mental to our tonal system in music today. Plato, Aristotle, Plutarch, Aristedes, too, equated health with harmony, and stressed the importance of music in achieving intellectual and moral "virtue" through a healthy interaction between mind (soul) and body. Aristedes further referred to music as being essentially a form of psychotherapy: "Music unites not only the individual in friendship with herself, but also promotes a mutual friendship among others." Asclepiades, Xenocrates, Celsus, Caelius Aurelianus and Boethius reported on the various ways in which music played a major role in cases of mental and nervous afflictions (Meinecke, 1948).

In the Middle Ages, disease was still regarded as a punishment and a sin, and many of the harsh and cruel measures employed for the treatment of the mentally ill were the reflection of the belief in demonology (Sigerist, 1944). "In Europe thousands of men and women who would now be considered insane were tortured, exorcized and killed, based on the judgment that their hallucinations or delusions represented a possession by the devil" (Stone, 1966). In contrast to the Greeks, who had regulated and controlled music as a function of the state for the ethical and moral growth of its citizens, the Church now assumed the task of molding the nature and use of music to avoid profane and pernicious influences on men's souls. This was an era of religious medicine. However, the teachings of antiquity continued to be practiced, particularly the belief in the power of the various musical modes to influence behavior (Boxberger, 1961).

Although the Renaissance inaugurated the modern age, it is the theory of the four humors, handed down by the Greeks, which becomes the point of direct contact between music and medicine at this time. The theory of the four humors, the corresponding four qualities of matter, and the resultant humoral pathology began with Hippocrates and prevailed for over two thousand years. It was based on the Pythagorean emphasis on the number four, consisting of two pairs of opposites, and on the cosmogony of Empedocles. The Empedoclean theory ascribed all material existence, animate and inanimate, to the various mixtures of the four elements—earth, water, air, fire. In medical theory, these four elements corresponded to the four humors of the body—blood, phlegm, yellow bile and black bile, and these in turn corresponded to heat, cold, dryness and moisture. Out of all this came the four temperaments—sanguine, phlegmatic, choleric, melancholic (Carapetyan, 1948).

This theory had an exact counterpart in the theory of music in the sixteenth century: it set forth four component musical elements and related them to the four cosmic elements. These musical elements were the four parts forming a complete harmony and, in performance, a complete sonority—the bass, tenor, alto, soprano. The bass was compared with the earth, the tenor with water, the alto with air and the soprano with fire. The analogy is completed when the four musical modes (scales) in use during the Renaissance are compared with the four cosmic elements and the four humors: here the four modes correspond to the four temperaments as well. Thus, the word "harmony" signified a bringing together of elements totally different from one another, whether in the cosmos, in the human body, or in music. Renaissance physicians also utilized music in the practice of preventive medicine; it was regarded as having a beneficent emotional effect which favored resistance to disease, a resistance that was threatened by the great epidemics of the time (Carapetyan, 1948).

During the Renaissance, interest was centered on man himself. The new emphasis on individualism, naturalism and in the achievements of antiquity were evidences of humanistic trends which eventuated in new approaches to the arts as well as the sciences. The growing exuberance and dynamic tension of the time lasted well into the Baroque period; they were reflected in the doctrine of *affections* which pervaded musical thought, the affections being the catalyst for change in the content of music. Instead of rendering a single affection, music began to encompass many contrasting emotions. This new emotional depth and introspective character aimed to convey man's inner passions and ideas; their complexities brought about the use of tempo and dynamic markings. Thus, music must be more than sensuous stimulation; it has to have expressive aims (Lang, 1941).

Beginning with the Renaissance, the rapid development of experimental physics, anatomy, and physiology, including research on acoustics and on the anatomy of the organs of audition, prepared the way for the seminal "Sensations of Tone" by Helmholtz, first published in 1860. Seashore (1928) sums up Helmholtz's contribution to musical psychology: "... every phase of vocal or instrumental music, artistic or inartistic, every emotional touch as actually expressed and conveyed by the musician can be represented by the four attributes of the sound wave; namely, the frequency, the amplitude, the duration and the wave form." Accordingly, "all music is a matter of sound waves which may be photographed and of sensory receptors and effectors which may be studied in detail by the anatomist and physiologist" (Diserens, 1948).

"The social and political reforms which followed the great western Renaissance produced changes in the treatment of the insane. France and Italy were among the first to provide so-called 'moral treatment', which attempted to preserve the humanity of the afflicted rather than to destroy the supernatural incubus. As retreats, hospitals, lazarettos, clinics and asylums were set up, large numbers of patients became available for study. ... In the 18th and 19th centuries physicians began to categorize mental patients on the basis of their symptoms" (Stone, 1966).

It is only since the end of the eighteenth century that the first objective efforts were made to evaluate the effects of music on the human body. Diserens (1922, 1926) has summarized this early work on the influence of music on functions such as circulation and respiration, on general electrical conductivity of tissues, on fatigue, and on general vibratory effect on the body as contrasted with the specific auditory response, as well as the effect of musical stimuli on certain externally observable reflexes. "Experimental studies of the effects of music upon our feelings confirm in part common experience and ancient tradition as to the effects of high and low pitch, varying intensity, different rhythms, and major and minor modes on our affective consciousness" (Diserens, 1948). He cites further studies which confirm a correlation of the emotional values in many musical compositions with definite moods.

The beginning of the Romantic school of composition in the nineteenth century is characterized by even greater intensification of emotional expression in music. Emotion, furthermore, has come to mean "personalized" emotion—the expression of the individual, which is associated with the use of dissonance. Music begins to bear the personal mark of its creator, whose personal emotional experiences and philosophy will be directly reflected in the music. The use of harmonic dissonance and rhythmic irregularity rapidly accelerated into the twentieth century (Hanson, 1948).

With growing knowledge and further discoveries in anatomy, surgery, bacteriology, biochemistry, neurology and psychiatry, scientific methods were incorporated into the treatment and prevention of disease (Sigerist, 1944). From the dawn of the scientific era in the nineteenth century, the decreasing use of music in general medical thinking and practice reflected a break between medicine and its philosophical roots in the past. It was not until changing circumstances a century later that music re-entered the treatment picture.

Music Therapy
in Hospitals

Music therapy is a hospital-developed practice; it evolved particularly in psychiatric hospitals, which have borne the major responsibility for the care of the mentally-ill in the United States for more than two hundred years.

From the outset, conditions in institutions for the mentally-ill were abysmal. One of the earliest indications of the abuses suffered by patients is that walls were finally built around the first general hospital in this country in 1760 to *protect the patients* from the gaping public, who came to bait and enrage them. The Pennsylvania Hospital began to charge a fee in order to limit the number of sightseers and, finally, banned the public completely by 1800 (Deutsch, 1949).

America was not spared the inquisition of ignorance originating in medieval beliefs in demonology. Some of the people persecuted as Salem's witches were in fact victims of a rare hereditary disease, Huntington's Chorea, brought over on the Mayflower by an affected family. This neurological disease causes movements of groups of muscles, and these movements were interpreted by the trials of persecution as possession by the devil (Stone, 1966).

Ironically, wars have been a major influence both in bringing mental illness to the fore, and in creating the means of attacking the problem. The Civil War helped establish the field of neurology, which advanced knowledge pertaining to diseases of the brain. During World War I, much resistance to psychiatry as an integral part of medical treatment was overcome. World War II spurred the devising of large-scale screening techniques, which are today applicable in other areas, as well as the establishment of the practice of group therapy; it also led to the greater use of music in hospitals.

Applications of music gradually evolved along four main lines:

1) *In Functional Occupational Therapy (FOT)*—During World War I, it was noted that many military patients recovered the use of wounded limbs sooner as the result of physical activities, especially during long hospital confinements. The purpose of FOT was to increase the functions of muscle power, joint mobility and coordination of movements. Re-training and coordination by special exercises were also necessary in the case of severe burns, and of nerve destruction

and disease. Music was prescribed as exercise for most of the joints and muscles of the body (through instrumental playing), and to increase the use of the lungs and larynx (through singing and blowing)—practices current to the present time.

2) *As an adjunct to psychiatric treatment* —Music was seen to have the following attributes in the treatment of mental illness (Gilman and Paperte, 1952):
   a) Ability to command attention and increase its span;
   b) Power of diversion and substitution;
   c) Capacity to modify the mood;
   d) Capacity to stimulate pictorially and intellectually;
   e) Capacity to relieve internal tensions;
   f) Capacity to facilitate self-expression;
   g) Capacity to stimulate resocialization.

Empirically-derived assumptions (Altshuler, 1944), (Altshuler and Shebesta, 1941), (Blackwell and Neal, 1946), (Coriat, 1945), (Isham, 1945), (LaMaster, 1946, 1947), (Robinault, 1949), (Simon et al, 1951) upon which its use has been based in most neuropsychiatric hospitals are:
   a) That rhythmic stimuli set up muscular tensions which seek immediate release through physical activity and which help, therefore, to pull the patient out of his morbid preoccupations and direct his attention toward things and events around him;
   b) That the moods created by different types of music stimulate emotional responsivity;
   c) That music awakens real or fantasied associations and memories and, in this way, facilitates the expression of repressed, unconscious material.

Authors such as Eby (1943), Hevner (1937), Simon (1945) and Van de Wall (1926, 1946) describe the ways in which music enhances and facilitates individual and group therapeutic activities. Some stress the socializing effect of music through vocal and dance groups; some emphasize the positive effect of mood change and physical release even with severe, chronic cases; still others see the development of musical skills alone as capable of giving new and stabilizing dimensions to the patient's life.

3) *As a direct aid to anesthesia*—When the phonograph was introduced into the general wards of veteran's hospitals during World War I, it was noticed that music not only entertained the patients; it also helped to relax them. Doctors introduced the phonograph into the operating room as a psychological aid at first. It was soon found that, as the patient relaxed while listening to the music, he could be anesthetized more easily and did not require the same amount of medication. In dentistry, too, its use was found to lessen the amount of anesthetic required, and to generally eliminate the administering of drugs for pre-medication.

4) *As a psychological stimulus in the total hospital environment*—Music was found to be especially effective as an accompaniment to meals,

calisthenics and remedial exercises; to increase the endurance and efficiency of work projects in the Occupational Therapy shop; to diminish anxiety and relax patients in the administering of certain shock therapies, e.g., when used in conjunction with hydro-therapy and electroshock therapy, Altshuler (1956) reported "synergistic facilitation"; to divert patients during time-consuming physical therapy and deep X-ray therapy treatment. Of course, music was indispensable as entertainment—at the bedside, in the ward and the assembly hall, or outdoors. In hospitals for the chronically ill, maximum enjoyment was obtained from listening to fellow-patients performing.

By the 1930's, the aim of the music program was to modify patient's moods, as well as destructive or immoderate physical activity, usually on the open ward. In this phase, the structural requirements of the group music activity provided the controlling framework within which the patient was helped to participate. With the introduction of the tranquilizing drugs in the 1950's, it became possible to utilize therapeutic approaches in greater depth to meet patients' psychological needs. By the 1960's, the two most commonly shared goals reported by practicing music therapists were: 1) The establishment or re-establishment of interpersonal relationships; 2) The bringing about of self-esteem through self-actualization (Gaston, 1968).

Before World War II, the U. S. Army provided for music by tables of organization which assigned a musician to small units. Until 1942, a band was provided for each regiment. During the war, however, music was discouraged, and only divisions and Armies were supplied with bands. Soldiers were not permitted to take musical instruments overseas during 1942 and 1943; nevertheless, many small varieties were secreted among organizational equipment—usually the mess (Ainlay, 1948).

When wounded men began to fill our hospitals, doctors were faced with the prevalence of functional disorders. They soon learned that music was not only a morale-booster; it was even more helpful as an adjunct to the recovery process. Music then became a part of the Army's Reconditioning Program; music utilized for physical reconditioning, educational reconditioning, and occupational therapy of the reconditioning program was administered under direct supervision of medical officers. (In general, audio-reception for recreational purposes was provided through the American Red Cross and other civilian agencies.) This was the first official recognition given to music as a specialized means to be used in military hospitals to help the sick and injured. For the first time, bands were authorized, not for marching purposes or military ceremonies, but for general hospitals. Shortly before World War II ended, music technicians were assigned to general and regional military hospitals to work directly with patients (Ainlay, 1948). This program exposed musicians and administrators to the potentialities of music in the hospital setting; it helped to increase the understanding of the functional uses of music, and led to the establishment of the music therapy profession.

In non-military institutions, the purposes, organization and control of music programs varied considerably from hospital to hospital (Van de Wall, 1948). In the mid-1940's, no criteria existed for the selection of the hospital music worker, or for the structure of a hospital music program.

Well-trained musicians and music teachers were not necessarily suited for hospital work: some fled the wards as too depressing; others were too upset by the manifestations of illness; still others were too frustrated by inconsistencies and set-backs in patient response, including learning and performance capabilities. Activities evolved from two extremes of the musical spectrum: from *individual teaching* at a patient's bedside, and from *performing* to large groups in ward and auditorium programs. Emphasis gradually shifted in each extreme—from the *individual* to the *group,* and from *passive* to *active.*

Group music provided one of the earliest and safest group experiences for the most seriously-ill mental patients; it furnished non-verbal persuasion not only to act, but to act together. Patients who could not enjoy any other form of common action beyond the bare fact of being near each other, could still sing or dance together. Even with increasing complexity of the activity, the feeling of belonging or "taking part" remained constant. According to Hughes (1948), group music necessitates a subordination of the individual to the group, a merging of individual desires in a common effort which is non-competitive and non-threatening. This subordination of self to the common musical good, in most cases, brings an automatic reward in the form of greater musical pleasure, and satisfaction and pride in group accomplishment.

In state mental hospitals, particularly, full-scale music programs were conducted on the ward and in large groups, in an effort to reach as many patients as possible. In this situation, the music itself produced involuntary responses such as clapping hands, sudden smiling, humming, singing or dancing, which often provided the opening wedge toward contact with reality and resocialization. Altshuler (1948) noted that many disturbed or confused patients responded to music either by tapping the foot, swaying the body, or nodding the head. When tempos were changed, corresponding changes were observed in these "thalmic reflexes." He, therefore, sought to strengthen this temporary contact through the "Iso" principle, which engaged the patient at his level of mood and tempo, and the ward at its level of volume and rhythm. Such applications of music have demonstrated the unique quality of music not only as non-verbal stimulus and modifier but, especially, its power to reach through the barriers of the withdrawn, isolated schizophrenic patient.

Through these applications, many patients were rendered accessible to other therapies for the first time. Group singing, square dancing and rhythm band (Shatin et al, 1961) activities assisted in arresting deterioration among chronic and senile patients; when utilized as tension-discharging stimuli on the wards, they helped improve interaction between patients and hospital staff (Lee, 1956).

In mental hospitals, we also learned of the patients' overwhelming need for satisfying experiences — in performance and in interpersonal relationships. These needs could best be met in a more selective way through small groups and individual sessions. Satisfying participation in musical activity for the patient depended upon the degree of his interest, the direct experience of successful learning and evidence of accomplishment, and the quality of his relationship with the music therapist.

From the point of view of the music therapist, the following factors appeared to contribute to the development of positive relationships with patients (Tyson, 1959): the degree to which each patient is perceived and considered individually, as a person whose feelings and sense of dignity are genuinely respected; the acceptance of each patient as s/he is, with whatever eccentric behavior s/he may present; the capacity of the music therapist for empathic response; the therapist's sensitivity and alertness to perceive and comprehend the slightest effort to communicate on the part of each patient; the extent to which the therapist participates dynamically in establishing communication, along with the use of music; the depth of the music therapist's conviction that the patient can learn and grow; the successful adaptation of musical concepts and materials to each patient's level of capacity.

Above all, we learned of the widespread motivational deficit which existed among patients suffering from a variety of illnesses, but particularly those with psychiatric disorders. Whether or not it was a consequence of constitutional breakdown, or a reflection of economic or cultural deprivation, this deficit very often existed prior to hospitalization. It existed, as well, among patients with musical aptitude or previous musical training.

The large-scale programs of music activities, then, were a means of stimulating response that might be kinesthetic, emotional, intellectual and associative, whether positive or negative. A function of the music therapist was to reinforce positive response in order to awaken or restore interest in music. This interest was then utilized as motivation for new learning and relationships, and reintegrating the patient into the social community. Where the interest was already expressed, the music-learning situation was usually regarded by the patient as a normal, non-threatening one in which he was willing to participate. Here the music therapist might function on deeper levels to achieve diagnostic, supportive and rehabilitative goals, depending upon a particular institution's philosophy and scope of practice. For example, the performance of music involves choices of instruments, choices of songs or musical selections, and choices of tone colors which may have diagnostic significance (Gaston, 1955).

A fully-developed hospital music program included the following activities: instrumental and vocal groups such as orchestra, band "combos," chamber music, chorus, rhythm band; ward community singing, music-listening and appreciation; ward and auditorium concerts; musical quiz, variety and talent shows; the staging of Broadway-type musicals; individual music study, including creative music-writing; folk and square dancing; religious choir; holiday pageants; maintenance and repair of musical instruments; construction of simple instruments; special ward and radio programs; programming music for public address system broadcasts; maintenance of a representative library of sheet music, records and books. Patients were encouraged toward maximum, appropriate participation in as flexible and informal a setting as possible. Sessions were usually no longer than forty-five minutes, and their musical content reflected the patients' preferences and interests.

Musical activity was regarded at first as a strictly recreational pursuit, and the major forms employed were instruction, performance and entertainment. Most often, the program was administered under the hospital's

Recreation Department, a practice which corresponded to prevailing custodial concepts of inpatient hospital care. In a further development, music was employed under the broadest interpretation of the meaning of therapy, which included the application of *educational* methods. Although not necessarily medically-prescribed, such methods were designed to counteract or terminate destructive processes and conditions favoring them. Through these procedures, the patient was seen as learning to collaborate with the various efforts of the staff to improve his condition by the use of his own physical and mental powers (Van de Wall, 1948). This shift in emphasis coincided with the growing trend toward *rehabilitation* and, in many cases, resulted in the transfer in administration of the music program to the Occupational Therapy Department.

The period after World War II experienced the cumulative impact of advances in social psychiatry, chemotherapy, and other related fields. At the same time, greater public interest and support resulted in increased state and federal appropriations for mental health services. These advances brought about a minor revolution in the management of mental patients; they made possible a dynamic shift in practice from traditional custodial care to the manipulation of the total environment for maximum therapeutic effectiveness.

In the mid-1950's, the effects of the tranquilizing drugs gave new emphasis and increased consideration to the usefulness of music therapy and, indeed, of all the creative arts therapies. For the first time, acute disturbed behavior among psychotics was modified to a large degree, which facilitated more normal interaction from patient-to-patient and from patient-to-hospital employee. Through improved social relationships, many previously inaccessible patients were able to take on deeper involvement with their immediate environment. (One of the important original uses of music as a mood-modifier has been largely eliminated since this time.) Hospitals began to mobilize all possible activities, music included, into full schedules designed to encourage growth processes and resocialization. The Activities Program developed at the Austin Riggs Center at this time, typified the growing belief in activity as a vital component of rehabilitation and recovery (Erickson, 1976).

But there was an even greater change which resulted from widespread use of the tranquilizing agents—a change implicit in their power to control acute states of anxiety and hyperactivity. It was now possible to return great numbers of patients to their homes and to general hospitals in their communities where they could be maintained on continued treatment at outpatient facilities. It was also possible to avoid hospitalization in many cases. These possibilities have become realities with startling rapidity. For example, during the past twenty years, the population in New York State mental hospitals has decreased from 93,000 to 24,000 and the downward trend continues.

Concurrently, these changes were reflected in hospital music programs. The broader applications became increasingly useful, whereas the high rate of turn-over, particularly among new admissions, precluded any meaningful continuity in working with individuals. This was frustrating for patients with strong motivation toward music and, for music therapists, represented lost opportunities of possible consequence in patients' rehabilitation.

Development of
the Music Therapy Profession

The National Association for Music Therapy* (NAMT) was founded in 1950, to foster the progressive development of the therapeutic use of music in hospital, educational and community settings, and the advancement of training and research in the profession. No formal college training existed before 1944. Today, there are close to seventy NAMT-approved academic programs offering an undergraduate degree, and twelve which offer graduate degrees. A six-month period of clinical training is required following the four years of academic work. NAMT members who complete a degree in music therapy or its equivalent from an accredited college or institution are eligible for registration (RMT). The Association and its Regional chapters hold annual conferences and workshops; the organization also publishes the quarterly "Journal of Music Therapy." An outstanding achievement has been NAMT's publication of Volume I of "Music Therapy Index", which covers the literature of the psychology, psychophysiology, psychophysics and sociology of music (Eagle, 1976). This has been followed by Volume 2 entitled "Music Psychology Index" (Eagle, 1978). A second national organization, the American Association for Music Therapy, was established in 1971 at New York University in New York City.

NAMT defines music therapy as the use of music to accomplish therapeutic aims: the restoration, maintenance and improvement of mental and physical health. It is the scientific application of music, as directed by the therapist in a therapeutic environment, to influence changes in disability or behavior. Since World War II, an increasing number of music therapists work full-time with physically and mentally handicapped children, with socially and emotionally maladjusted adolescents and adults, as well as with geriatric and mental patients and the physically handicapped, in hospitals, clinics, day care facilities, community mental health centers, correctional institutions and special service agencies. There are increasing openings in state and federal institutions under civil service. Public schools are beginning to employ music therapists as members of special education staffs working with exceptional children, particularly if they are also certified as music educators. Some RMT's work privately with patients referred by psychiatrists and other health professionals.

*P.O. Box 610 Lawrence, Kansas 66044

What are some of the evolving concepts which have contributed to growing applications of music therapy?

Music, as a form of human behavior, is closely related to the behavioral sciences, and requires knowledge of man's nature and development to be adequately understood. The understanding of *music therapy processes* depends upon a multidisciplinary approach, which takes into account biological, psychological and cultural influences on the behavior we call music (Gaston, 1968). It is of interest that the condition known as *amusia* (lack of correlation of behavior with respect to musical stimuli) is classified as a pathological phenomenon (Revesz, 1954).

Sears (1968) proposes a theoretical formulation for the processes of music therapy; its integrating focus is the behavior of the individual when involved in a musical experience. The three underlying classifications are: (1) Experience within structure; (2) Experience in self-organization; (3) Experience in relating to others. His use of the word "music" refers to musical situations, although it may have any of four designations: the music itself; listening to music; having music in the environment; the making of music.

Great emphasis is placed on rhythm as the most dynamic element in music (Gaston, 1968). The simplest and most basic effect of rhythm is to synchronize and regularize movements; another effect is to center attention upon itself rather than upon the effort of moving to the rhythm. The stimulus of rhythm invariably produces motor, muscular or glandular responses (Diserens, 1948). Muscular responses of the listener and their emotional concomitants suggest the importance of rhythm in determining audience response (Hughes, 1948).

Rhythm has been called "the language of physiology" (Hudson, 1973), and an absolute lack of it is difficult to find in nature. Nature being full of periodicities (Luce, 1970), and our bodies exhibiting a series of natural rhythms — heartbeat, respiration, brain waves, peristalsis, etc. — it has been supposed that our pleasure in musical and other rhythms is based upon the degree to which they harmonize with and facilitate our physiological rhythms (Diserens, 1948).

Sounds and rhythms are among the innate sense hungers which need to be satisfied if normal growth and development are to take place (Gaston, 1968). Rhythm may be one of the earliest and most inherent pleasures, possibly originating from the sound and movement in the environment of prenatal life. Lullabies are strikingly alike the world over; their chief characteristic is regular, monotonous, rocking rhythm (Gaston, 1968). Infants and children respond to joy and to stress with rhythmic, repetitive action—from head-banging and rocking to spoon-banging and marching (Luce, 1970). It is notable that most music of adolescents is similar in regularity to the rhythms of prenatal and infant life (Gaston, 1968). Graham (1958) found that anxious and fearful patients would be much more likely to join in group rhythms if tempo and rhythmic pattern were kept constant, whereas they would not if the rhythm and tempo were changed often.

The experimental literature on the feeling effects of music deals with its influence on moods, the feeling value of melody, rhythm, pitch, loudness, tempo, timbre or tone color, the major and minor modes, and with musical preferences. There is striking consistency among normal persons in the recognition and acceptance of *moods; personal preference ratings* and *semantic-associative* responses reflect broad inter- and intrapersonal fluctuations. Fine research on the human voice carried out by Seashore and Schoen touches upon the psychology of phonetics and speech (Diserens, 1948).

Among more radical or detrimental affective responses have been cases of "audiogenic" seizure (Reese, 1953), where convulsions have resulted in response to music despite the clear absence of organicity. Daly and Barry (1957) and Joynt and Green (1962), reporting on cases of musicogenic or "affectogenic" epilepsy, attribute the attacks, not to the musical stimulus itself, but to the particular susceptibility and build-up of emotions in the subjects while listening to the music.

From the psychodynamic point of view, music is regarded as a language which gives symbolic expression to unconscious contents and strivings. It is nonthreatening because it "represents the good object, which loves and therefore is loved" (Racker, 1951). The sense of hearing is capable of appealing directly to the emotions: "In respect to crude sound, hearing is similar to the sense of smell ... largely repressed in civilized man, yet retaining its powerful early affective bonds" (Knapp, 1953). Langer (1953), writing from a philosophical viewpoint, regards music as a symbolic language through its *form,* not its *content:*

"The tonal structures we call 'music' bear a close logical similarity to the forms of human feelings ... (thus) music is a tonal analog of emotive life."

Music and language are thought to share a common archaic origin (Ehrenzweig, 1953). According to Noy (1967), many psychoanalytic investigators assume that, since music is a language lacking in objects and conceptualized content, its origin antecedes that of spoken language; it may therefore originate from pre-verbal stages, i.e, periods in which primary thought processes were still prevailing, when the clear separation of the self from objects had not yet been achieved. Some authors believe that the very structure of music is based upon the model of the primary processes, and that a study of musical structure will yield deeper knowledge of the primary processes themselves. Still another group of authors believe that music stems from a defensive need for either control or dominance of specific primary experiences, e.g. threatening auditory perceptions, occurring during the first stages of life.

In a more recent related development, Bernstein (1975) sets out to prove the existence of a "worldwide, inborn musical grammar." Utilizing techniques borrowed from the modern study of linguistics, he finds analogies between musical phrase and nouns, between harmony and descriptive adjectives, between rhythm and verbs, and describes how these are transformed into the structure of music. He concludes that there is a "universal" musical language whose source is the *harmonic series.*

Twentieth century psychiatry has been dominated by Freudian psychoanalytic theory, which is concerned with "intra" psychology, an individual-oriented view of inner conflict. Therapy is a verbal process which consists of uncovering repressed material in the individual's unconscious, usually through the technique of free association and dream interpretation. Psychoanalysis differentiates three levels of functioning in the psyche:

1) The instinctual forces or drives called collectively the ID (which can be related to emotional experience);
2) A psychological center of organized experience, synthesis and mastery, the EGO (which can be related to art or play);
3) The core of internalized restrictions imposed by outer authority (parental, educational, cultural, moral), the SUPER-EGO (which can be related to music as work and aesthetic experience (Braswell, 1962).

The therapeutic efficacy of musical activity at each of these levels depends upon the capacity of music to repeat an emotional conflict in a medium that is relatively free from conflict (Kohut, 1952). For example, music not only facilitates the release of fantasies "but may also serve as a substitute for the fantasy ... when repeated in humming or whistling" (Sherwin, 1958)—all providing added dimensions for therapeutic exploration.

An outgrowth of the Freudian movement, of major importance to music therapists, was the development of *milieu therapy* at the Menninger Clinic in Topeka, Kansas during the 1930's. Under this concept, the usual recreational and occupational therapy activities, music included, were utilized in a new way; they were analyzed for their inherent therapeutic values and, at times, prescribed much as drugs (for example, for gross motor activities to release hostility). For the first time, the music therapist became a primary agent in the treatment of patients. S/he was required to know the patients' medical and social background, as well as the treatment goals. Activities were guided by psychiatric prescription and staff consultations. Milieu therapy gave the adjuvant therapies a valid theoretical framework in which to operate, and helped create an identity for them in the psychiatric profession.

The use of prescribed activities with emphasis on *relationships*, marks the beginning of the "inter" phase of treatment in modern psychiatric hospitals, wherein relationships between patient and therapist, patient and patient, and patient and group can be assessed and utilized (Braswell, 1962). Within this context, music facilitates social interaction. By its very nature, music draws people together for the purpose of intimate, yet ordered, function; it provides a gestalt of sensory, motor, emotional and social components in which the participants generally concur. It unites the group for common action, and it is this setting that elicits or induces changes in many extramusical behaviors (Gaston, 1968). The cooperative efforts of the combined staff represent the *psychiatric team* concept. The team forms a psychological and social circle around the patient, and each member, including the music therapist, provides a source of psychological stimulation for the patient, who is the center of all measures taken (Van de Wall, 1948).

The emergence of the professions of social psychology and group dynamics, with their emphasis on the etiological and therapeutic potentials of groups, has also provided new and important theoretical constructs for music therapists (Braswell, 1962).

Although developmental theories are based upon the study of child-hood, they are of pertinence in our work with seriously-ill adults, who frequently function on many varying levels. It is helpful for the music therapist to be aware of the emotional, intellectual and behavioral aspects of psychosocial development, in order to more effectively deal with the "child-in-the-patient."

Erikson stresses the creative and adaptive power of the individual. His major focus is the nature of the ego processes—play, speech and thought. These are the *adaptive* manoeuvres to influence inner and outer forces. In contrast to Freud, who considered the study of dreams the road to the adult's unconscious, Erikson (1963) submits that play, which involves self-teaching and self-healing, is the ego's acceptable tool for self-expression and mastery. Certainly, the playful, improvisational possibilities in music are manifold for ego-oriented goals.

What are some of the music therapy techniques which are receiving widest application?

1) *Developmental Music Therapy (DMT)*

The DMT program is based directly upon the Developmental Therapy (DT) model in existence at the Rutland Center in Athens, Georgia. DT is a psychoeducational approach to therapeutic intervention with young children who have serious emotional and behavioral disorders, particularly between the ages of two and eight years. The shift to a childhood education setting involves the translation of traditional music therapy practices into a therapeutic approach based upon patterns of sequential growth and development.

The DMT program offers a series of music therapy experiences designed to complement and enhance the DT curriculum. The model reflects contributions from the professions of psychiatry, social work, psychology, education and music education. DMT establishes therapeutic goals in the four curriculum areas of *behavior, communication, socialization* and *academics*. The four areas are organized into five developmental stages which require certain behaviors of the music therapist and the child at each stage. Each child progresses at varying rates through the developmental hierarchy within each curriculum area. The music therapist's role, the amount of intervention required, the type of simulated environment and music experiences needed, and the amount of participation change with each stage (Wood, Graham et al, 1974).

2) *Nordoff and Robbins' Improvisational Music Therapy (IMT)*

In their work with handicapped children, the authors employ a highly sensitive, mercurial technique involving improvisation and musical interaction; the child's incipient responses are encouraged as a means of activating inherent normal capacities. There are thirteen categories of responses according to which a child's behavior may be explored, eight of which concern rhythm and drum-beating behaviors. Vocal responses are of primary importance with children who have no speech: crying or screaming become crying-singing (tonally related to the music), which then becomes singing.

Improvisations are utilized to awaken emotional responses at the level of the child's fragmented, disorganized psyche. Emphasis is on expressive and creative freedom within the musical experience and from the self, and the pleasure derived therefrom. There is free use of dissonance in improvisations. These experiences enable younger children who are involved in processes of inner differentiation and growth, to develop and consolidate ego-organization.

With growing freedom and expressiveness, the child's awareness expands to include the music therapist as the source of his music and the stimulator of his responses. Through and within active musical experience involving playful give-and-take and musical-dramatic forms, the child engages in a co-creative process with the music therapist. The growing unity of the emotional-musical bond leads to a sharing and working together, and to a completely new human relationship for the child. The central motivating power of music therapy is seen as the child's commitment to his musical activity (Nordoff & Robbins, 1972).

3) Guided Imagery and Music (GIM)

GIM is an outgrowth of the search for mind-expanding techniques which could produce "altered states of consciousness" (ASC). Clinical research conducted with high doses of hallucinatory drugs aimed to facilitate insight and bring about peak or transpersonal experiences in the psychotherapeutic treatment of alcoholics, narcotic addicts, terminal cancer patients and neurotics. It was found that the most meaningful results were obtained from a sequence of appropriate music in combination with psychedelic drug-assisted psychotherapy (Bonny and Pahnke, 1972). During its eight to ten hours of duration, music played a significant part by: helping the patient relinquish usual controls and enter ASC more easily; helping to bring out hitherto repressed emotions and feelings; directing and structuring the procedure in a non-verbal way; contributing toward a peak experience.

Because of anti-drug publicity, the black market and dangers of improper drug use, a therapeutic approach was sought which could give similar results without the use of drugs. The GIM technique was developed, roughly based on the psychosynthesis model of Roberto Assagioli, involving four levels of mind: the lower unconscious; the unconscious; ordinary consciousness; the supraconscious or transpersonal. Physiological and psychological behaviors—from primitive and pathological to that of creative insight and higher order drives—originate at these levels. The process consists of expanding awareness of self into both upper and lower levels of consciousness; when observing and dealing with the lower level's symbols and images, the self can begin to work on unresolved personal conflict (Bonny and Savary, 1973).

The GIM techniques begin with standard procedures of induction which include relaxation and concentration as a prelude to listening to specially selected taped music, in the presence of the therapist.

Eyeshades and earphones are employed to help guide and direct the experience. Audio tapes are designed for areas of response such as the following: Beginners Group-Experience; Affect Release; Positive Affect; Comforting/Anaclitic; Death/Rebirth; Peak Experience; Quiet Music; Cosmic/Astral. Music facilitates ASC through sensory bombardment which can reach many levels of consciousness; the subject may be carried from one state to another or, sometimes, to several states at once.

4) *Clinical Orff Schulwerk (COS)*

This approach, utilizing the method of music education developed by Carl Orff for German school children, has been specially adapted for mentally retarded and autistic children in the United States (Hollander and Juhrs, 1974). COS offers an effective groundwork for these children because of their pre-disposition toward rhythm, order and repetition. The overall process involves the use of movement, rhythm, sounds, language and musical expression in a group experience. Structure is provided by the simple chants, rondos, poems, nonsense words and ostinati employed, all sung within the pentatonic scale. The rondo form is used extensively, as it allows for repetition as well as for individual creative response. Specially-designed percussion instruments permit the participation of even the most severely disturbed or handicapped child.

Through "successive approximation," specific tasks are taught in a concrete step-by-step approach. Learning is effected through modeling (imitation) and behavior shaping, reinforced by behavioral techniques (Ponath and Bitcon, 1972). With groups of autistic children, considerable attention is given to language development through the use of sign language (adapted from American sign language for the deaf), which is seen as enhancing speech. Among other areas dealt with in the Orff context are body image and awareness, laterality, gross motor expression, fine motor coordination, receptive language, spatial relationships, simple categorizing and simple association. The significant value of COS is that it helps the child to become invested in a meaningful group experience (Hollander and Juhrs, 1974).

5) *Application of Behavioral Principles*

Although not specifically derived from music therapy, behavior modification techniques are widely applied in music therapy and special education settings for retarded and emotionally disturbed children: the goal is to reduce interfering behaviors and increase learning. "Such behaviors include not following directions, short attention span, self-destructive behavior and various stereotyped behaviors" (Jorgenson, 1974). Contingent music activity paired with social reinforcement are effective in reducing such interferences and raising the level of participation.

The positive approach to behavioral change is stressed. Treatment plans assess a child's strengths and difficulties, and pinpoint the behavior to be learned or changed. Techniques involve observation, recording, reinforcement and shaping.

Clinical Orff Schulwerk is an example of a music-based approach which successfully incorporates behavioral principles.

6) *Application of Kodály Concepts*

Kodály's pedagogical concepts are closely related to music therapy concepts, especially in working with emotionally disturbed children. The Kodály method is based upon the use of Hungarian folk and game songs; it emphasizes relative solmization, rote-learning and "inner hearing" (mental rehearsal). There is a thorough acquisition of performance skills long before concepts are introduced.

The process begins with simple two-note songs, usually within the pentatonic scale. Rote-learning is facilitated by movement, hand signals and visual aids. Physical closeness, touching and eye-contact are an integral part of the approach. The child gains security through repetition, gratification through enjoyment, and the satisfaction of participating and relating in performing groups.

Kodály's concepts involve a sequence of graded learning. The problem of adaptation, which is in process, lies in the transformation of these concepts and their related learning sequence from Hungarian folk music to American folk music, which has its own distinctive properties and content (Lathom, 1974).

7) *Psychodynamically-oriented Music Therapy*

Utilizing this viewpoint, the patient is not only helped to discover strengths but to deal, as well, with the manifestations of deeper unconscious problems as they arise within the music-learning situation. The focus may be on the patient's interpersonal behavior or on his musical behavior. When these manifestations or patterns persistently interfere with the patient's musical goals, the music therapist directs the patient's attention to possible underlying causative factors. Invariably, the interaction with the music therapist reflects the patient's emotional adaptation to a significant parental figure and it may also become helpful for this transference to be clarified. Under conditions of a "split transference," the music therapist must be able to work in close collaboration with the primary psychotherapist toward beneficial outcomes for the patient.

However, orthodox psychoanalytic principles no longer dominate the psychotherapy scene; as long as they did, transference was regarded as the *only* operative relationship, and there was no place for music or art. "The need for expression other than verbal, and the growing conviction that relatedness is one of the decisive features in human life provides the place for the therapeutic use of music and art" (Boenheim, 1968). The therapist moves from the position of analyst to that of ally and active supporter who helps the patient to learn, to mature, and to grow emotionally by working through problems on a more realistic level. Boenheim (1967) calls this phase of treatment "synthetic," in contrast to the analytic approach.

Progress depends upon an understanding of psychodynamics, which emphasizes a sequential development of personality, and the role of unconscious motivation with regard to personality function. The concluding study of Kathy described in the section entitled "Case Studies" typifies this orientation.

8) *Psychiatric Musicology*

This approach applies musicological methods to the stylized music patterns of chronic, regressed patients. Analogies exist between the altered forms of patients' perceptions and their behaviors. When repetitive stylizations are brought to the attention of patients, are discussed and their explanations accepted by the therapist, more satisfactory reorganizations in music frequently are achieved, with subsequent spontaneous improvement in patients' speech and behavior. Perceptive errors are also discerned in patients' artificial speech intonations and in their hearing of the music of others. Inappropriate responses bear a consistent correlation to patients' altered perception of a situation.

Clinical information, useful in diagnosis and treatment planning, is based upon "formal analogies between details of the structure of music and of interpersonal events, rather than on any content equivalency" (Stein and Euper, 1974).

Music Therapy
in the Community

The re-entry of psychiatry into the community (Branch, 1964) made it possible to develop music therapy as a community-based rehabilitative modality.

The music therapist's range of influence and responsibility increases as he moves from the hospital into the community (Tyson, 1968). Hospital music therapy is usually highly departmentalized and functions as one of many adjunctive services in a total treatment setting. Out of practical necessity, there tends to be greater emphasis on music *activity* rather than therapy. The fact that the hospitalized patient is sheltered and supervised at all times, and is concurrently being seen by medical, nursing, social work and other rehabilitative services, also shelters the music therapist.

It is essential to realize that music, of itself, or musical proficiency alone, do not account for growth processes; change takes place within the context of a therapeutic relationship. Out in the community, therefore, more important even than musical competency, is the actual or potential wisdom, maturity and capacity for therapeutic effectiveness on the part of the music therapist. No amount of musicianship, training or education can help bring about behavioral changes in others when one is closed to change in one's own behavior. Little of therapeutic significance will occur unless the music therapist has the ability to empathize and communicate nonverbally (Ruesch and Kees, 1956), and the capacity to enter into a responsive relationship and to consciously use the resultant interaction to induce emotional growth processes in the patient.

It is also helpful to bear in mind that the hospitalized patient tends to respond in a more passive way than the outpatient, who more readily questions or challenges the music therapist's role and may even attempt strenuously to pit the music therapist against the primary psychotherapist. Unless the patient's initial skepticism and conflicts are handled in such a way as to alleviate them, the patient may feel unable to continue music therapy. Another distinction is that the hospitalized patient is a relatively "captive" participant, whereas the patient in the community will expend the time, the effort and the money only if music therapy is experienced as meeting the individual at the level of his/ her needs.

What are the needs to be met? There is the patient's tenuous hold upon reality, which results in a precarious, unstable day-to-day life situation;

the inability to formulate goals or to apply oneself with sustained energy; low self-concept, which perpetuates destructive and self-defeating tendencies; lack of satisfying experiences; profound misunderstanding and distortions of events and responses. There are overwhelming fears and anxieties arising from the many complex life problems to be faced: housing, income, family relationships, vocational training or job-seeking, schooling, dating or, even, a dental appointment. Above all, there is the terrifying isolation which results from the inability to relate to others.

In our highly automated, technologized and computerized age, "normal" man has become depersonalized and alienated from himself and others. The suffering of emotionally-ill people is compounded because their conflicts and problems have already had the effect of isolating and alienating them from themselves and from others. Many are so withdrawn that they are simply unable to communicate freely or adequately on a verbal level. Also, for some, words are frequently used as a smokescreen which veils and distracts from the truth of feelings and thoughts (Tyson, 1973).

For the emotionally-ill patient who is attracted to music, it may offer the only bridge from inner world to outer reality. It may provide the only means to give expression, in a safe way, to inner feelings. Particularly in the outpatient situation, where there is no continuous supervision of a patient's behavior, it is important that the music therapist's sphere of interest be the inner life of the patient — that the main concern be with the use of music as a vehicle by which this inner reality can be brought to the surface, to be heard, experienced and examined in the presence of another.

Members of the wider professional community may hesitate to refer their patients to a separate music therapy resource. The hesitation often reflects an unwillingness to "pinch off" patients from the primary treatment milieu and expose them to an independent ancillary service that might interfere with, or operate at cross-purposes to, the ongoing basic therapy. The music therapist should be equipped to function with greater psychological sophistication in the community, because there is a wider range of emotional disability to be treated than one encounters in hospitals. Many of the patients have never been hospitalized. These include individuals suffering from the psychoneuroses, or from behavior and character disorders, who are frequently rather psychologically aware and literate as the result of receiving private psychotherapy or analysis. The primary therapist may be a Freudian, Jungian, Adlerian, Reichian, Sullivanian, hypnotherapist, bio-energeticist, lay therapist, group practitioner, etc. The music therapist must be able to comfortably and effectively work with them and their patients at their widely differing levels of functioning, awareness, and psychological and treatment orientation.

In the community, music therapists have to contend with closer working relationships with patients who, in attempting to make their way in life, are frequently more upset or volatile or threatened than their counterparts in the hospital: there is the increased possibility of savage verbal attacks or of impulsive acting-out behavior; there is the frantic telephone call or visit because the patient's psychiatrist is away or cannot be reached; there is the telephone call late at night threatening suicide; there is the recurring powerful impulse that the patient may experience to drop psychotherapy and discontinue music therapy. Needless to say, it is *not* good music therapy to deflect the patient from nonmusical concerns and problems which s/he feels the need to discuss; such a response would be construed as rejection. What assurance is there that the music therapist can cope with the more extreme possibilities inherent in the new situation?

The answer lies in the realization that music therapy is not an end in itself, and that the simple transfer of the departmental operation as it functions in hospitals does not suffice. Music therapy acquires deeper dimensions as a community practice. At times, it may become the "central" and most important element in a patient's therapy (Zwerling, 1979). The music therapist must become more aware of the patient as a whole person, and of the fact that each one-to-one contact has possible immediate and crucial implications for the patient's total life situation (it is not merely a question of adjustment on a sheltered hospital ward). It is the *constant impinging of total reality on the music therapy contact* which creates the necessity for a broader framework—dynamically and socially oriented — within which music therapy can best serve the outpatient's needs (Tyson, 1968). Occasionally, the outpatient situation may require a commitment involving direct environmental intervention in the lives of the patients referred.

The community music therapist should meet regularly with a consultant psychiatrist. There are many situations which arise, and many problems encountered in working with patients which require airing, clarification and guidance. Consultation needs may revolve about questions of transference or counter-transference, the setting of limits, personal defenses, prejudices or characteristics which interfere with the development of a positive therapeutic relationship, disagreement with the referring psychiatrist's point of view, or an incomplete understanding of the behavioral dynamics involved in a particular case. It is incompatible with the adjunctive nature of music therapy that the music therapist work against the instructions of the primary psychiatrist, even when s/he is privately in disagreement with them—or that s/he unwittingly add to the patient's confusion or ambivalence—or that s/he be taken in by any of the patient's resistance to psychotherapy or, for that matter, to music therapy. These are eventualities which can be clarified, rectified or minimized through regular consultation.

Among the questions which community music therapy raises are (Tyson, 1968): How can the music therapist successfully work with a patient when the referring agency has provided insufficient background information (to protect confidentiality, sometimes the diagnosis is indicated merely as "mental illness")? What happens with the patient already in music therapy who is suddenly without a psychiatrist (as in the case of the ex-hospital patient who has been discharged from the state aftercare clinic, or of the patient who is in the process of switching from one doctor to another)? Should there be an automatic cut-off date for the term of music therapy? What are the criteria for terminating a patient from the music therapy program?

Exploratory projects undertaken at the first psychiatric outpatient facilities in New York City revealed that the newly discharged mental patient who is interested in music or who has had music therapy while in the hospital is not at all ready to cope with regular academic demands (Tyson, 1957). S/he still requires a sheltered situation which affords the opportunity for successful learning and participation; without it, the interest in music is apt to lead to discouragement and defeat, with possible deleterious consequences.

In the late 1950's, community rehabilitation programs emphasized social, recreational, educational and vocational goals in a group environment. There is no question of the usefulness of music activity in a social or recreational program. However, many of the most musical outpatients disassociated themselves from these general group activities: they craved more individualized and personalized work and relationships. In the difficult post-hospital phase, many patients suffered the lack of sustained, supporting relationships and of opportunities for ego-strengthening. It became apparent that the encouragement of individual musical capacity and interest as a source of health (Fisher, 1958) awaited the availability of a separate music therapy resource in the community.

Creative Arts
Rehabilitation Center, Inc.

Among the new services is Creative Arts Rehabilitation Center (CARC), also known as Music Therapy Center (MTC), in New York City. The Center is a nonprofit, nonsectarian organization—a social rehabilitation agency for emotionally-ill adults and children who are in psychiatric treatment in the community. CARC functions as a therapeutic community (Jones, 1953) whose common language is the arts; here music, dance, art, drama and poetry therapies are utilized as adjunctive modalities to promote emotional and social growth, in accordance with medically prescribed goals. The only requirements are a high response or interest on the part of the patient, and referral by a treating psychiatrist or psychotherapist. Although music probably has some significance in a patient's history, previous musical training is not a criterion. The central program offers music therapy through the medium of instruction in a wide range of instruments, voice and theoretical subjects. In addition, patients are encouraged to participate in arts-centered small group activities, when they are ready. As far as the patient is concerned, there is no curriculum, there are no tests, there is no time limit and there is no pressure. As each patient receives individualized attention, the possibilities of competition, threat or failure are minimized. Liaison is maintained with the referring psychiatrist or agency throughout the course of music therapy, either by direct contact or written progress reports. Over 165 psychiatric clinics, hospitals and rehabilitation facilities, in addition to private psychiatrists, are utilizing this service.

In hospitals, a major overall goal is the resocialization of the patient, with the music therapy department helping to remotivate the patient toward this goal. The same overall goal is served in the community: the music therapy operation is transformed into a total milieu operation—an agency for the advancement of social rehabilitation. While the rehabilitation objectives which have been prescribed by the patient's psychiatrist continue to be served in individual weekly sessions, there is also the overriding intention to stimulate and implement interaction among the patients referred (Tyson, 1968). The Center's experience demonstrates that the goal of socialization cannot be realized when the music therapy program consists of a single music therapist having consecutive appointments. As the number of patients increased, two or three music therapists were scheduled for concurrent but staggered sessions, and social interaction began among patients in the waiting-room. The opportunities for interaction gradually expanded with the addition of other creative arts therapies and of groups to the program.

At CARC/MTC, the therapeutic intention takes precedence over music-learning considerations. This is evident in two ways: in the awareness of creating a total environment conducive to promoting emotional and social growth, and in the awareness that while the music therapist is working to develop an individual's musical capacities, his primary concern is that this experience contributes to a more mature level of functioning in the patient's total life situation.

Thus, the environment is consciously "open" (although not lacking in necessary firmness and structure)—its character is informal, warm, permissive and highly personal. The filled candy-pot on the waiting-room table is not an accidental symbol of the program's intention (Tyson, 1965). Since 1962, in this relatively unprotected setting, there has been a remarkable absence of aggressive or destructive behavior; rather, an ever-growing response has been noted in the sense of belonging — in the patient's identification with the Center and with those who attend it, as well as with those who work for it. The only precept which is enforced is consideration and respect for one's own rights and the rights of others (this applies both to patients and staff).

The music therapist, like the teacher, is concerned with the learning process, with skill in communication, with promoting the growth of pupil-clients toward reality and maturity. Like the teacher (Highet, 1950), s/he must know his subject well and believe in it; s/he must care about people and be able to maintain satisfactory relationships with them. Unlike the teacher, however, the music therapist regards his subject as a tool, as a means of achieving objectives which aim at influencing behavior and adjustment. Whereas the teacher-pupil relationship is teacher-centered and based upon the pupil meeting the standards and expectations of the teacher, the music therapist-patient relationship is patient-centered and based upon the therapist meeting the emotional needs of the patient.

In an article, Dr. John H. Fischer (1962), dean of Teachers College, Columbia University stated: " . . . formal education is always a deliberate cultivation. The principal source of energy the teacher uses in the process is the dynamic power of the student's growth and maturation." This source, this power, is not readily available in the emotionally-ill individual, in whom it has become arrested or deflected. Unlike the teacher, it is the province of the music therapist to deliberately cultivate growth and maturation, not so much through the patient's possible love of learning as through the *love of music*. At the same time, the therapist is strengthening the existing healthy parts of the patient's personality.

Another distinction involves the basic sensory capacities, which are largely inborn and tend to be elemental. The young child has the sense of tone quality, of volume, of rhythm and of consonance long before s/he begins to sing or know anything about music. In normal musical training, it is the *meaning*, and not the capacity, of these senses which we train and which matures with age in proportion to the degree of intelligence and emotional drive (Seashore, 1938). Not so with the emotionally-ill person whose sense hungers have been starved, thwarted or inhibited: the music therapist works with that part of the sensory apparatus involving sound and rhythm—to restore the innate capacity to perceive pitch, loudness, timbre and pulse.

The underlying approach is the freest possible gratification of instinctual aims through the medium of music. These aims include immediate satisfaction, pleasure, joy (play), receptiveness and absence of repression (Marcuse, 1955). Their greatest gratification derives from the freest possible "outflow." This reinforcement of the pleasure principle may at times appear to be a regressive measure in terms of the music, but it is regression "in the service of the ego" (Kris, 1952). Under the control of the music therapist, it allows for the release of current tensions while fulfilling infantile yearnings. It requires foregoing academic considerations, and taking as many (musical) steps backward as may be necessary to impel the first involuntary steps forward.

> For example: A middle-aged woman was referred for piano sessions. She had had extensive training through the college level, and was an accomplished pianist. This patient lived at home, still bound to her mother in a destructive, symbiotic relationship. Her demeanor was polite and dutiful; her movements were rigid and puppet-like; her affect was at all times bland and flat. For several years, she attended the Center for weekly sessions, during which she rushed through a fairly advanced classical repertoire as if skating on ice—all renditions were totally devoid of feeling or differentiation of any kind. She offered no opening, not an iota of communication, either verbally or musically—not until an unexpected change brought her in touch with a new, younger therapist, with whom she felt an immediate rapport. Thereafter, this patient chose to play progressively simpler pieces, until they were actually at the beginning child's level. Gradually, elements of warmth, playfulness and spontaneity began to be expressed in the course of the developing new relationship, which the patient evidently perceived as more accepting and less threatening.

Once these steps are taken, at the patient's pace, and if they are fully shared and accepted by the therapist, to meet the patient's needs, then the prospect of forward (musical) movement becomes possible. This is the pre-condition for growth and learning, and for the patient's eventual acceptance of the reality principle, with its attendant restraints.

To achieve outflow is by no means simple in patients overwhelmed by guilt, immobilized by anxiety or engulfed by the tides of self-destructiveness. In such cases, gratification acts to increase emotional tensions, and the patient must defend himself against it by denial, inhibition and reaction formation. Outflow is an aim that must be carefully and gradually encouraged as the patient warms and expands, and attains greater trust, ease and relaxation. It also does not depend upon technical accomplishment.

At times, the outflow may be nonmusical in character, as when it represents the release of hostile feelings. Many patients who express the need to scream or pound or beat are unable to do so directly; ways must be found to provide an outlet within a musical context—ways that are not frightening to the patient or damaging to his self-esteem. The scream is incorporated at the apex of an ascending vocal scale; a solidly chorded or turbulent forte passage in a piano score presents an opportunity for repetitive pounding (Tyson, 1965). Invariably, the patient communicates the need for such an outlet, but not always verbally. Both patients and music therapists tend to be somewhat timid about the use of music in this respect. It is more than likely that a therapist's reluctance stems from the possibility that the violence inflicted upon music is a threat to his/her own defenses. The patient will generally not make the attempt unless s/he feels the wholehearted encouragement and approval of the therapist. The music therapist must not be satisfied with tentative efforts, but should ultimately lead the patient through ever-louder and more intense repetitions until signs of relaxation (deep breathing, dropped shoulders, loose hands and arms) indicate that release has been achieved. The patient obtains satisfaction from the combination of kinesthetic elements with the symbolic, as the action is destructive of music itself. It is important never to end such a session before guiding the patient back to sublimating musical activity. At no point can there be any doubt of the therapist's ability to control the extremes of emotional expression.

The character of the sessions is determined by therapeutic considerations—they do not necessarily resemble music "lessons." A patient may enter the studio, carefully adjust the chair before the piano keyboard, place the music on the rack and then proceed to talk of the week's problems, all the while subtly resisting any attempt to work with music. Or a guitar may be painstakingly tuned, only to provide a background of strumming for a stream of conversation. Such behaviors are accepted as an indication of need, whether arising from a pressing reality situation or a desire to test, or as a defense mechanism. Considerable latitude is allowed to the point where the patient himself would have to agree to the lack of musical progress; all the while, gentle but timely pressure is exerted toward the musical activity involved. If the pattern persists, it is discussed with the referring psychiatrist or, possibly, dealt with directly.

Sometimes, when a patient appears to be in the depths of despair or depression, the therapist may offer to play a favorite piece of music, making no other demands. This "gift" seems to have inestimable restorative power, with its unspoken values of sharing and caring. Or, a "musical conversation" may take place, with the patient playing as s/he feels, and the therapist answering musically in kind. Upon occasion, art, movement, eurhythmics, dramatic play, "conducting" and improvisation are incorporated into the sessions.

It is central to the CARC program that patients be drawn into musical *activity* — that they *make* music — by playing an instrument, singing, humming, dancing, composing or conducting. Patients are helped to make music in the area of their choice, at whatever emotional or performance level they present. Despite the fact that many patients seek out music therapy because of the action element involved (the accent on doing things responds to the demands of our time, according to Boenheim, 1967), this confrontation by the necessity to *do* is often an anxiety-evoking prospect for the new referral. It involves self-disclosure, and the patient fears that the revelation of his/her inadequacies or feelings will invite ridicule and rejection.

For many patients, it is an ordeal simply to come to the Center—to manage the right transportation for themselves, to face new people, to expose themselves to the possibility of failure in an activity close to their hearts. As one caseworker reported:

"Miss B. is practically a recluse in her furnished room . . . she stays at home engaging in ritualistic physical exercises for hours a day, writing prose and poetry which she usually destroys—often oblivious of the passage of time. Weeks of preparation were necessary before she would venture to make her first appearance in the Center. Additional help was needed so that she would not retreat again when instruction on the accordion was unavailable. It is a great achievement for Miss B. to come even though sometimes late to a new setting to sing in the presence of another person."

Upon receiving a new application, an appointment is made to see each patient for what can best be described as a "music-centered" interview. The initial contacts are conducted in a manner to convey reassurance, acceptance and receptivity. The interview, itself, is intended to epitomize what the program stands for, by providing the patient with an experience of what s/he can hope to expect from it. (One patient remarked: "This isn't an interview; this is therapy!") The object of exploration is the patient's life experience in a number of areas: in music (or other art form indicated); in education; in employment; in hospitalization(s) and/or therapy; in social relationships; in goals and hopes; in creative endeavors and hobbies; in self-estimate of problems and strengths; in present and early family relationships. The feelings and perceptions of the total human being—not of the "patient"—are being elicited. The interviewer's comments are directed towards establishing consonances and similarities with his/her own experiences or that of others. As notes are taken, they are read aloud (as if to check for exactitude) in order to allay the patient's anxiety or distrust. There are practical reasons, not solely financial, for inquiring about job status and living arrangements. This information may uncover obvious frustration factors, such as the unavailability of an instrument or of practice facilities or the necessity that sounds be muted, and may suggest the wisest immediate choice of instrument (Tyson, 1965).

Therapeutic considerations, especially parental attitudes, influence the assignment of a patient to a music therapist. Occasionally, the sex of the therapist has already been specified among the psychiatrist's directives. An attempt is also made to "match" personalities, whenever possible, according to depressive, extrovert/introvert and creative/imaginative characteristics in order to facilitate rapport. If, subsequently, a therapist's personality or color or physical anomaly creates a barrier or threat which the patient is consistently unable to cope with, then a re-assignment is effected.

The preliminary music therapy sessions are exploratory, both of the patient's personality and musical potentialities. It is necessary to discover what is acceptable, to minimize resistance and anxiety. Most often, a patient's strong interest in music coincides with some degree of natural endowment or talent. Those with the greatest endowment of musicality seem to derive the greatest gratification from music itself, despite emotional problems. Even partial endowment or functioning provides gratification as, for example, in a patient with highly sensitive aural perception who may be inhibited or poorly coordinated in the area of rhythm. The starting point, or base for new learning, is the area in music in which the patient experiences the greatest gratification. Thus, the music therapist begins on the conscious level, with the healthy components of the patient's personality; s/he seeks the individual's propensities and strengths in relation to music, to demonstrate them, reinforce them and build upon them. As newfound strengths are noted, they are related to the patient's life situation (Tyson, 1965).

Incidentally, high musicality is not an automatic indication for successful music therapy, as conflicting values may lead the patient to ignore this aptitude and seek fulfillment in other areas. The Center has worked with patients of average or low musicality in whom all that could be discovered was a single positive quality in relation to music, such as the capacity to sing on pitch. Yet this single attribute is revelation enough to build feelings of self-worth and self-assurance strong enough to result in markedly improved emotional stability and adjustment. The building of such feelings applies as well to individuals who may have had extensive prior musical training.

There is a basic discipline which guides the music therapist in the course of the relationship with the patient: it is the consciousness that one's every word and gesture may have therapeutic implications of which one may be unaware. No matter how informal and relaxed the attitude or how sincere the warmth and interest, the relationship must never become personal: one offers skills and support objectively, to help the patient regain or acquire the inner strength to meet life's challenges independently. In the writer's opinion, these objectives are more reliably attained if the music therapist has had at least three years of personal psychotherapy.

The experienced music therapist: provides "invisible" guidance whenever possible by favoring an indirect approach over direct means to enable the *patient* to arrive at the next connection, realization or insight; is not uncomfortable with silence, and chooses to wait rather than to proceed impulsively; would rather listen than tell; knows when and how to employ a bit of humor to break the tension of a trying moment.

Very often, we work to keep a patient in basic psychiatric treatment by helping the person to understand *process* —the nature of *resistance* and how it arouses uncomfortable, almost unbearable pressures. With such assistance, we find many patients are enabled to withstand the tensions of this phase of basic therapy. Sometimes, the turning point for a patient occurs at a time of deepest frustration and negativism, after s/he has tested and provoked the music therapist to the limits of endurance. There comes a point when the music therapist "rolls up his sleeves" and must establish and affirm his belief in the particular patient's rights to a worthwhile and self-realizing existence. In a sense, the patient has been begging for this; the cues have been building up for quite awhile. This type of session is not usually marked by reasonable, verbal discussion; rather, it is a testing of strengths more in the form of a confrontation. The patient is hoping that the therapist will win, but s/he fights stubbornly and fiercely against it.

Or, it may happen that a patient who is an accomplished pianist will choose to discontinue the instrument in favor of simple recorder playing, in order to participate in the instrumental group. This occurred to a middle-aged woman who had studied piano for eighteen years. She was extremely anxious, chronically dissatisfied with life, dominated by competitiveness and hostility, yet overwhelmed by feelings of defeat and hopelessness, as her potential had not been realized. This progression to the recorder was encouraged, as it served the resocialization needs of the *whole* person.

Nevertheless, in spite of and because of these functional approaches to patients' problems, because there is emotional and social growth of the patient at the Center, there is almost always musical growth (Tyson, 1973).

What are some typical *musical* behaviors which may indicate emotion-based causality? Among such responses are: absolute refusal or inability to play from notation (defiance of authority) which is frequently converted into the motivation to play by ear; insistence upon playing from note-to-note instead of grasping the entire musical phrase (lack of confidence; immature clinging to the security of the known); tendency to rush tempi (early parental pressures); inability to tolerate contrary motion in counterpoint (fear of conflict); necessity to play "all loud" or "all soft" (overwhelming hostility or denial of hostility); inability to play by ear (blockage, inhibition arising from restrictive, controlling upbringing); melodic or rhythmic constriction (overwhelming stress in infancy); uneven rhythm (fear, confusion or conflict regarding sexual drives); when playing by ear, over-reaching or under-reaching in attempting to reproduce intervals sounded by the therapist (anxiety due to distrust, suspiciousness, feelings of inadequacy); emotionless renditions (dissociation from feelings; fear of letting go of feelings). In working with patients referred to the Center, the parenthesized "causes" have occurred so frequently as the contributing factors as to suggest more than accidental or superficial correspondence to the musical problems involved.

For example: a 22-year-old man was referred to CARC with the diagnosis: "Psychoneurosis marked by depression and tension." Fred characterized himself as a "loner", and had dropped out of graduate school because of increasing bouts of nervousness and suicidal thoughts. He distrusted all emotion and tended to rely upon intellectual defenses. He was self-taught upon the recorder, which he played in a stiff, mechanical way.

The music therapist always started each session with: "Well, what would *you* like to do today, Fred?" This usually threw him; it wasn't the way he believed his world was structured. One of his problems had been finding out just what *he* really wanted to do. In this one, small situation, then, he could begin to throw off some shackles; it took him some time to stop trying to second-guess the music therapist, and determine what *he* should be doing, not what *she* might want him to do.

In the course of nineteen music therapy sessions, Fred discovered that emotional inhibition predisposed him to choosing Baroque pieces, because he regarded them as being devoid of feeling. He discovered that, underlying his preference for familiar music, was a strong need for security. He discovered that he was clinging to the visual prop of printed notation, in order to evade the deep anxiety which accompanied his attempts to play by ear. Music therapy helped this patient to integrate his emotions and his intellect by using them both to produce music, and it helped him to take pleasure in the expression of his emotions.

This patient wrote: "Playing the recorder with my music therapist and with some of the other members at the Center has been a relaxed and pleasurable achievement. I think it is the first goal I achieved just because I wanted to, just because it means something to me, just because it has something to do with the way I want myself to be. As such, it has become the model for the way I hope to live my life."

At the Center, we have also seen that there is considerable justification in reality for the frustration and anxiety which many of the most musically-educated patients have developed. Histories of instrumental and vocal instruction reveal that many were subjected in their early years to a one-sided teaching approach which rigidly and joylessly emphasized rote-learning for the sake of technical proficiency. The lack of preparation in musicianship resulted in insecurity and immaturity in their musical experiences which were further intensified by growing emotional problems.

The touchstone of the patient's early progress lies in the combination of the gratification s/he derives from music and from the quality of the relationship with the music therapist. Providing the patient with a continuum of small successes leads gradually to a more hopeful outlook regarding the expectation and enjoyment of success. As trust and confidence develop, the patient gains the courage to discard old ways, and becomes more receptive to new learning. At such times, new musical insights permit the replacement of entrenched habit-formations with new patterns of reaction and response. It is far more difficult to work through this phase with patients who have already received musical training, as they tend to cling to previously learned musical patterns and misconceptions. This process of self-confrontation, the discarding of old ways, and the adaptation to more successful functioning in relation to music activity cannot be considered educational in the academic sense; it is the outgrowth of *re*-education in living.

As for the question of music pedagogy, there does not appear to be a single approach or particular system which can meet all music therapy needs. It appears more efficacious to permit each music therapist the freedom of his own musical approach, as long as his basic training is sound in these areas. With the goal of facilitating immediate satisfaction, materials and methods may be shaped by the individual therapist's flexibility and ingenuity to bypass anxiety- and tension-creating elements. Many innovations arise from the need to develop concrete representations for abstract musical ideas. Devices such as numerical or alphabetical notation, lateral notation, numerical patterns or shadow-playing may be universally used, but they are not universally applicable or acceptable— each patient presents an individual problem and, frequently, an uneven or erratic training background. Despite good results, patients may require reassurance that these devices are not childish and do not reflect unfavorably upon their intelligence (Tyson, 1965).

Group activities were initiated at CARC, at the patients' urging. Two Musicales are held each year in which the majority of patients willingly participate, without concern for level of accomplishment. These events have resulted in strikingly improved socialization and interaction, and led to the formation of a variety of arts-centered small groups which meet regularly once a week—groups involving drama, singing, recorder ensemble, chamber music, music-listening, rock music, percussion and poetry. There is also a monthly Performers' Workshop. A foreign-born patient who participated in many Musicales wrote: "What a way of creating a pleasant gathering of people united, maybe every single one in a different approach, but in a pure love of music. Who wants to can perform, without any form or thought of competition. That is what I love about it." Thus, the course of the Center's development is being shaped by the needs of the patients who participate in its program; it will undoubtedly also be shaped by the growing demands for service from the outside community—not only from psychiatric agencies but from those concerned with the retarded, the aged and the physically handicapped. Professional needs add their impress, too, both from the point of view of advanced training of music therapists and of establishing a basis for research.

Successful rehabilitation "requires a coordinated effort by many professions, agencies, and community resources" (Black, 1963). This requires communication with practitioners in varied disciplines: psychiatrists, lay analysts, psychologists, social workers, vocational rehabilitation counselors, school guidance counselors, nurses, activity therapists, and others. Occasionally, the Center has initiated a referral to another agency, e.g., referral to a vocational rehabilitation facility may be indicated when a patient appears to have a persistent employment problem which has not received specialized attention. When collaborating with other agencies, meaningful communication is facilitated by a realistic "mutual awareness of the needs and subsidiary goals of other participants on the team" (Clausen, 1956). It has proven helpful to be active in the programs of closely related professional organizations, in order to increase our understanding of their concepts and goals.

Upon occasion, patients are referred to the Center just prior to discharge from hospitals. In such instances, it is desirable that the referral be completed by each patient's psychiatrist or social worker, rather than by the hospital music therapist. In this way, more adequate diagnostic and case history material is provided and channels are established for direct supervision and guidance on an outpatient basis. However, the Center's therapists and those in the hospitals communicate with and assist one another as much as possible in planning treatment in the community for these patients.

Just as, in hospitals, music therapy prepares patients to utilize other prescribed therapies, so does it facilitate the vocational and social rehabilitation of the musically motivated outpatient referred to the Center. The intrinsic nature (Williams, 1953) of the activity itself provides the opening wedge to emotional and social growth within the music therapy setting which, in turn, carries over to other settings. This includes progress in individual psychotherapy, adjustment in the home, and improvement in interpersonal relations. In a number of instances, the threat of being dropped from the Center's program has been persuasion enough for patients to remain in psychiatric treatment during particularly difficult phases.

As for the unique contribution of music therapy in facilitating the release of repressed memories and feelings, it would seem that the commonality factor—the mutual sharing of interest and love of a safe third object (music) — helps reduce the authoritarian component in the therapist-teacher role and permits a more equal and direct interaction. In many cases, the closer relationship, combined with the pleasurable nature of the activity, acts to minimize the elements of threat in the situation and loosen the patient's habitual safeguards.

Much of the realm of practice at CARC lies in *pre*-educational, *pre*-occupational and *pre*-socializing areas; it incorporates many of the elements of "guidance" which emphasizes support and clarification, and the "reduction of the ego load through communication and objectification" (Slavson, 1964). The process involves guided preparation which is, first of all, unstructured and nondemanding in relation to the activity, which provides a permissive atmosphere and a relationship based upon unconditional acceptance. It involves identifying strengths and talents, as well as supplanting the self-defeating mechanisms which invariably impede the patient's *musical* progress. Sometimes, it also involves instances of abreaction, as when a patient suddenly re-lives a heretofore repressed traumatic experience. At such times, it is helpful for the music therapist (while fully aware that s/he is not the primary psychotherapist) to be well-enough equipped to help the patient achieve some insight into his reactions and behavior, so as to relieve the accompanying anxieties.

In no sense, could the majority of patients referred to the Center have engaged in avocational pursuits to any constructive or satisfying degree. As most are blocked in one way or another by inner conflicts and their various defensive manifestations, as well as by environmental stress, it is these very reactions which must frequently be dealt with in relation to the music-learning situation. This is accomplished as the patient begins to identify with the music therapist, whose supportive attitude enables the patient to accommodate to more relaxed super-ego demands than s/he had previously incorporated, thus reducing the severity of his inner conflict. The resulting release of the patient's ego strength with the liberation of bound-up energies, helps to increase the patient's motivation and capacity toward the activity. The music therapy situation is, therefore, also essentially *pre*-recreational; the patient is realistically ready to put leisure hours to constructive use at the point of terminating music therapy (Tyson, 1966).

Case
Studies

The following five studies of intensive music therapy, condensed from individual session reports, illustrate the work being done at the Creative Arts Rehabilitation Center by three different music therapists. They are in no way intended to convey a belief in music therapy as a cure-all, but they do attempt to describe the content of sessions and responses which seemed to result exclusively from music therapy.

1. *Michael*

The following study describes the effects of music therapy as the specific modality employed to improve a young patient's adaptation to life within the limits of deteriorating organicity (Ludwig, Tyson, 1969). Research provided little empirical data since both pediatric and psychiatric literature are notably barren regarding the question of catastrophic illness (Morrissey, 1964). For the therapist confronted with progressive disability or premature death, it was necessary that, as Connor (1964) suggests, there be a reordering of values away from product orientation and work ethos toward a position of primary concern for the total child and his attainment of self-realization.

In the music therapy situation, changes in behavior or adaptation can rarely be entirely attributed to the effects of music therapy itself. The very nature of the Creative Arts Rehabilitation Center program requires that each patient be in regular psychiatric treatment and that he be referred by his psychiatrist (Tyson, 1966). In addition, there has been a proliferation of services available to patients in the community, so that frequent overlapping occurs—of individual psychotherapy, group psychotherapy and, possibly, participation in a social rehabilitation facility or in other activity therapies. These concurrent forms of treatment are not necessarily under the supervision of the same psychiatrist. Thus, while the various treatments may reinforce and actively support one another, it is unusually difficult to isolate the contribution of one adjunctive therapy in particular.

A psychiatrist referred his twelve-year-old son to the Center with the diagnostic description: "Brain-damaged, Aphasic." The following rehabilitation objectives were indicated: stimulate resocialization and interpersonal communication; provide reassurance and support; build self-esteem; strengthen reality contact; allay anxiety and fears; increase verbalization; develop concentration and attention span; encourage independence. The psychiatrist also requested that particular attention be paid to carry-over, if any should occur.

Michael B.'s history constituted an unusual record of contradictory diagnoses stemming from the baffling nature and multiplicity of symptoms manifested; it was notable because of the courageous and persistent search of informed parents for a meaningful diagnosis and because they were in a position to consult the most highly qualified professional experts available.

The early developmental history was well within normal limits. At 3 years and 2 months, regressive symptoms appeared, including loss of speech, decreased comprehension, poor sleep patterns, rocking on all fours, return of wetting and soiling, and deteriorating contact with the environment. He was occasionally seen closing his eyes and rubbing his forehead while rocking, screaming and crying — as if he might have a violent headache. Shortly before these behavioral changes, the child had had a bout of what was tentatively diagnosed as whooping cough accompanied by slight fever and, 4 months later, an acute tonsillitis with high fever.

At age 4, Michael was admitted to a large urban medical center for evaluation and diagnosis:

Neurological impression: "I don't know whether this child's difficulties are primarily physical or psychological. I would favor the former without sufficient evidence to do so. Of the organic disease processes that are possible, Heller's disease is one possibility.

Psychiatric impression: "My own impression of the boy was, although he presented the picture of a psychotic type of disturbance, there was much to suggest the possibility of an organic CNS disturbance and that the diagnosis would be probably clarified with the passage of time. The EEG findings were not strongly in favor of organic disease."

Psychological impression: "The overall impression is that of childhood schizophrenia."

Speech and Hearing evaluation: "This child shows the clinical picture found in patients with damage to the language centers—transcortical aphasia—which in this case may be part of a progressive disease of the central nervous system invading all areas of function and behavior."

Official diagnosis at discharge: "Undiagnosed disease of the nervous system manifested by deterioration of speech and behavior."

Recommendation: The patient should be in therapy. He was discharged home to be followed by lay therapy under the supervision of a psychiatrist.

Confused by the diversity of opinions expressed by the hospital specialists, the parents sought an additional opinion from a psychoanalytical colleague, who declared that there was no organic condition and that the basic problem was emotional. Following the recommendation of both hospital and outside psychiatrists, Michael was then seen several times weekly by a lay therapist. After eight months of psychotherapy, the following psychodynamics were suggested:

The child has an overdeveloped super-ego leading to extreme shyness and stubbornness through over-identification with his father. The states of recurrent confusion are due to manifestation of rebellion against early toilet training. All these factors have created an exaggerated dependency of the child on the mother.

The supervising psychiatrist, however, was inclined to give more importance to two emotional experiences which could have been traumatizing:

1) Fear of a cat which jumped on the child's bed one night;
2) Castration fear induced by seeing a little girl naked.

At this time the child developed a persistent cold, lasting for a period of several weeks, which was accompanied by periods of daze, irritability and daytime rocking, the child again giving the impression of a reaction to headaches. The parents sought further evaluation (at age 5) at another major urban medical center, which stated:

"It was our combined impression that we were dealing with a child who presented the general clinical picture of an autistic child with special lability in the biological areas manifested by severe allergic disturbances."

At age 7, a speech therapist was consulted and reported the following impressions:

"...his difficulty with boundaries and consequent diffuseness interferes with appropriate responses to his environment. There seems to be little stability in perceptual or conceptual experience. Behaviorally, he is disorganized, aimless and bizarre. Orientation of self in space is at a primitive level."

In the same year, Michael was taken for psychiatric re-evaluation to the major urban medical center where he had been seen two years before:

"... although some progress has been made, he still presented most of the classical features generally associated with the autistic child. However, there was evidence at this time that he was emerging from a total state of autism and had begun to develop early object relationships with beginning symbol formation and acquisition of speech ... it was quite obvious that many extensive emotional problems in parent-child relationship existed that could be identified as having some significant relationship with the overall clinical picture seen in the child. During my own contact with the child himself, I could not identify any specific neurological problems."

As the result of a pediatric neurological consultation at a New England hospital, the following impression was obtained:
"Cerebral dysfunction, convulsive disorder. Anxiety intense."

The educational history of this child was tailored to the requirements of the varied diagnoses, with the result that he attended schools for normal children, for autistic children, for aphasic children, and for children with behavioral disorders. Since his fifth year, Michael had attended five specialized schools. He also had three private tutors, two of whom were highly qualified in special education techniques for the brain-injured. The parents report that up to the time that music therapy was begun at age 12, no real concepts had developed.

At this point, the father, as a practicing psychiatrist, referred his son to Creative Arts Rehabilitation Center. Because of the boy's consistently high response to music noted since infancy and despite his accelerating deterioration, the father hoped that music therapy might provide a modality through which communication and learning could be effected.

In appearance, Michael was an attractive, well-built boy. He smiled readily but often inappropriately. He seemed mildly distrustful and rejected all body contact. He had excellent motor skills and good motor coordination. However, his movements were subject to disruption at any time by sudden freezing in the midst of action or by unpredictable outbursts of violent activity. He had no spontaneous speech. He displayed severe echolalia and perseveration.

Because so many of Michael's impairments seemed to revolve about the lack of conceptualization—difficulty in associative thinking and encoding processes (Kirk and McCarthy, 1961) — the encompassing goal was to establish and strengthen associative thinking and internal language. The therapeutic aim would be to implant language patterns derived from musical materials—language patterns embedded in the matrix of rhythm and melody. Hopefully, these patterns would serve as the bridgehead toward communication and speech.

The immediate approach was two-fold:

1) To facilitate interplay as the pre-condition for change by meeting the patient at his differing affective and operational levels;
2) To establish trust (Erikson, 1951), initially through nurturing and permissiveness, as the pre-condition for age growth.

Among the developmental discrepancies presented, the inability to utilize auditory stimuli consistently contributed to the patient's distractibility and inattention to speech. However, his high responses to music made it possible to focus his attention by creating meaningful auditory experiences through music. Songs and song games were chosen and created which initially provided infantile language play on the level of babbling, involving lip play, plosives, and long drawn-out vowels. On the other hand, the rhythms were strongly marked and rather complex to match the greater maturity of his motor development.

Once Michael's attention was focused, the immediate goal was to elicit communication on any level. At this time, the boy's general feeling tone was one of passive acceptance, illuminated at rare moments by flashes of resistance. These negativistic impulses were exploited toward the formation of the first definite non-verbal communication. His resistance was verbalized and labelled by the therapist. By further encouragement and acceptance of the negative response, verbal communication was effected. Michael's first word in music therapy was NO and, through it, he began to be able to perceive his identity and establish autonomy. He was next encouraged to assume control of the sessions: he had to choose between two songs or two activities, and his decisions were respected.

Positive verbal communication—YES—proceeded from new-found ego strength and positive feelings. Once it was identifiable on a conscious level, it was but a short step to eliciting the verbal YES through song patterning. The folk song "John the Rabbit," with its strong rhythms and built-in statement-and-response sequences, was a useful starting point and it helped to initiate interchange (Seeger, 1948).

Association proceeded from patterning, and was the first step towards increasing Michael's understanding of the world about him. The words of song patterns, such as in "The Train is Acomin'," were related to movement cues, to visual cues and to auditory cues. As always, the appeal was through pleasure. Slowly, the words began to acquire stable meaning. Michael would listen intently and strain to follow the therapist when she attempted to increase associations beyond those already firmly established in a loved song. Thus, with stimulation provided by pleasurable experience through the medium of sound, a secondary reinforcement process took place as the sounds themselves acquired more pleasurable meaning (Mowrer, 1952).

Constant repetition was necessary to establish language patterns, and repetitious folk songs provided the ideal medium (Ludwig, 1957). Changes were kept to a minimum, because of their threatening and disruptive effects. Words and phrases were repeated over and over, and procedures were strictly adhered to until the response became consistent. When the child had the security of a well-established response, the possibility of change was introduced (Isern, 1965).

Feeding was deliberately incorporated into each session as another and more primitive form of communication. Every session included a feast of gumdrops or a few mints. At first, Michael greedily crammed the food into his mouth without discrimination. He slowly moved from stuffing himself to selecting his favorite, feeding one to the therapist, and saving one for his mother. These more mature patterns were acquired by direct imitation of the music therapist, and were reinforced in the home. Michael was taken to the supermarket daily, where he learned to choose one item which he would serve as a family treat. Again, he gradually moved from the infantile satisfaction of choosing his own favorite to a more mature desire to please and surprise his parents by occasionally choosing their favorites.

As previously mentioned, Michael's history included many unpredictable outbursts of violent activity which resembled explosive temper tantrums or rages. These outbursts were often preceded by an interval of sharply increased motor activity and tension. During music therapy, the point of onset of an attack (or "motor aura") appeared when he would begin to hum to himself, paying less and less attention to melody and rhythm so that the melody became telescoped. At these points, his voice was loud, he articulated well and he sang more words and phrases. He also seemed out of contact, rocked himself and wrung his hands incessantly. When the therapist intervened by singing the same song, marking the rhythm strongly and holding the phrases back, the upward spiral was retarded or prevented on a number of occasions. This intervention was introduced at the patient's accelerated output level and gradually reduced to the accustomed tempo of the song. On a somatic level, vigorous ball-playing (an inflated beach ball) to strongly rhythmic song-games also helped to dissipate tension at the onset of an attack, as it provided kinesthetic reinforcement of the perception of the beat.

Michael attended the Center for one and one-half years, during which time his worsening condition continued to be evaluated and re-evaluated.

During the last 9 months of music therapy, Michael developed difficulty in swallowing and motor weakness on the right side. The boy was subject to increasing spasmodic "seizures," which he appeared anxious to try to ward off or control. (Gradually, the seizures became constant and began to involve his entire body.) The number of interruptions during sessions caused by body contractions, large tremors, shudders, grimaces, explosive grunts, blinking and staring left him exhausted.

Paradoxically, although the seizures were an overwhelming physical burden, he was more interested and alert than ever before. Learning was taking place.

It was possible to begin playing the piano together, with Michael "shadowing" the therapist. From simple shadowing of the melody one octave higher, Michael began to anticipate notes and play them alone. He insisted upon increasing his field to two octaves so that he could play the C chord in the left hand, in imitation of the therapist. His attention span at the piano increased from several minutes to a half-hour. There was more verbalization, more singing, more volume and improved recall. Above all, he was obviously enjoying himself and obtaining great satisfaction from the awareness of success.

In the course of eighty-nine music therapy sessions, communication was established, which made it possible for Michael to open up contact with those about him. There was notable diminution of hyperactivity and increased affect and control of its expression. More activity was now conducted on the conscious level, with very little of the bizarre stereotyped behavior (smelling, tasting, touching, etc.) which had been originally presented. Motivation had developed from the primitive gratifications of food and play to the higher gratifications of achievement and increased effectiveness. From an undifferentiated view of self and world, Michael appeared to be attaining a more coherent perception of himself and his relation to his environment.

Although the original referral requested that the Center pay particular attention to carry-over from week to week, the following communication received from the parents eloquently indicates the extent of the carry-over:

> Behind our child's deficit has been discovered, through music therapy, hidden resources which are helping him to lead a happier and more dignified life.
>
> The first general improvement noted was the clarity in meaning of positive and negative—*yes* and *no*. When asked if he wanted an orange, he began answering with decisiveness either *yes* or *no*. When he was able to do this, he began to know what *yes* and *no* meant when said by others. In a very general way, he began to comprehend more fully the usefulness of certain activities in the home and to contribute to them.

There is an extraordinary improvement in comprehending and relating abstract factors. 'Up,' 'down,' 'high,' 'low,' 'slow,' 'fast,' are now meaningful. 'Stop' and 'go' signs, after years of patient efforts of highly qualified teachers over many years, became meaningful only through music therapy.

We have noted a new generosity and pleasure in giving. There is also an increase in incentive. Previously, he could very seldom choose an activity, although he would willingly participate when offered a specific activity. Now he goes to the kitchen cabinet and takes pleasure in choosing a snack; he goes to his closet where his toys are kept and chooses one to play with.

His social behavior has changed. He greets friends at the door and brings them things he wants to show them. He will dance with people, although he still does not like to be touched unless it is a teasing game or a playful push, which he loves.

One last word about the music therapy sessions—Michael floats home from them as though he has just had a marvelous experience.

The main concern of Michael's psychiatrist was to increase the life experience of this child, and help gratify his normal desires, so he might better cope with the world as he found it, for as long as he could function in it. Through the application of music therapy as an educational modality, it was possible to utilize this patient's life-long attraction to music as a pathway to communication.

2. *Dennis*

A 27-year-old professional musician, a drummer, Dennis H. was referred for corrective breathing and voice placement by a psychiatrist who had recently begun to treat him in individual and group psychotherapy (Tyson, 1966). This patient was suffering from anxiety neurosis and presented many somatic complaints: frequent headaches, stiff neck and choking; the sudden sensation of faintness and ensuing fear of blackouts which he experienced daily; severe gastrointestinal discomfort which awakened him many times each night. He slept a great deal, rising later and later every day, and would often nap in the afternoon. On the days when he went to the union to seek work, he felt handicapped by inability to sustain his speaking voice and was plagued by frequent hoarseness and laryngitis.

Dennis was singularly tall, pale and slender. His ears seemed very large in contrast to his narrow, thin face. His gaze was indirect and somewhat furtive because of crossed eyes. His stance was that of a thoroughly defeated old man: his head thrust forward from stooped shoulders over a caved-in chest, all forming a backward arc from his protruding stomach. He walked in a flat-footed manner, with toes pointed sharply outward.

Dennis' behavior was characterized by distrust and verbal hostility which took the form of sarcasm and compulsive criticism. He had no close friendships with members of either sex. He was unable to tolerate criticism from anyone — acquaintances, family, employers or colleagues. There were corresponding problems in his professional life: severe anxiety attacks before going to work; fear of blacking out while drumming;

somewhat uneven tempo variations; an intense feeling that he was being used as a scapegoat by the soloists, conductors and other members of the various bands he played with. In general, he was keenly aware of a lack of direction in his professional and personal life.

Above all, this patient experienced an over-riding sense of anxiety stemming from three accidents which had occurred at the ages 14, 16 and 21; in the first two he had suffered relatively minor fractures, but in the last, an automobile crash, his neck was whiplashed and he suffered severe compound skull fractures. He had undergone plastic surgery and a painful, long recuperation. Ever since, he had had a feeling of weakness and had lost all motivation. He was living in constant worry over the fragility of his head, and in fear of possible brain damage.

In the course of the first music therapy sessions, Dennis was very rigid and tense. He couldn't yawn, he couldn't feel the root of his tongue with his thumb or touch the temporomandibular joint or try to drop his jaw; he resisted rolling his head back and, in fact, resisted doing the prescribed exercises. These reactions obtained even though he was eager and well-motivated; he strongly felt that breathing held the key to his development.

Shortly thereafter, the patient started a session by recounting the story of a heretofore forgotten childhood accident on a small merry-go-round and said it was probably the reason he resisted doing anything with his head or neck. As he told the story, Dennis began to sweat profusely; he seemed overcome by emotion and at the point of fainting. The accident had been caused when the little girl who was riding with him inexplicably and without warning dismounted at her end of the revolving apparatus, which upset its balance; Dennis had been violently thrown from his seat, knocked unconscious and badly injured at the back of his neck.

Suddenly, as he was speaking, Dennis became completely rigid and lost all awareness of his surroundings. He screamed in terror and agony as he lived through the automobile accident which had occurred 12 years later when he was 21. He again experienced all the sensations he had felt as the car spun slowly around, as it crashed into the telephone pole, as he came to on the street in the nightmare reality of debris and blood, again with painful injuries to the head and back of the neck. He broke into sobs (of self-pity, he later said) when he realized the similarity to the merry-go-round experience, both out-of-control situations. A description of this music therapy session at his next psychotherapy appointment led to a second abreaction of the automobile accident, which was then dealt with in depth. The patient today feels that the aural elements involved in both traumatic events (the ticking of the merry-go-round's gears and the screech of the automobile's tires) linked them together and predisposed them for emergence in the music therapy situation.

There were, of course, deeper unconscious elements which linked the two experiences together in a more potent and meaningful way and, although the music therapist tried to avoid dealing with these directly, awareness of them helped to facilitate the course of music therapy. Dennis felt considerable constriction in the genital area, related to the traumatic experiences. Consequently, the early sessions emphasized the develop-ment of lower-abdominal breathing, in order to provide an elastic yet secure foundation for later training in diaphragmatic breathing. After he had attained a good grasp of lower-abdominal breathing, its use was limited to the first exercise at every session for it toned important support-ing muscles and freed the patient's body from tension and constriction.

A short time later, in the course of breathing and placement exercises, the patient noticed that he kept losing breath at the crucial point. The music therapist remarked that he *permitted* it to happen — that he had shown a pattern of retreating from exertion and effort. The patient said this was just what happened with girlfriends if he thought one preferred another male—he would give up and run away. He said he had the same sinking feeling at his diaphragm — the feeling of collapse — about girls, when the music therapist urged him to try to stand fast and hold onto his breath throughout the next exercise. He tried many devices to avoid and procrastinate but, finally, succeeded in doing several exercises for the first time with complete control and a feeling of mastery. He was overjoyed, as he recognized the implications of what he had done.

During the next six months, the patient progressed rapidly in many ways. The music therapist provided the first positive relationship he had ever experienced with a woman and gave the support which helped him make his first real attempts to break with his overprotective but castrating mother; he gradually acquired insight into his occasional hostile outbursts during music therapy sessions, both as to their causes (rejecting and critical immediate family, aunt, schoolteacher) and present effects (social isola-tion, justification of his further antisocial behavior, and of masking to forestall anxiety). The music therapist helped the patient to identify his musical and related personal strengths and sources of satisfaction which, much to his surprise, led to the discovery that he wished to become a teacher above all things in life. With his self-esteem rising, this patient was beginning to act with markedly decreased hostility and self-destructiveness.

At this time, several fruitful sessions followed consecutively:

One day, Dennis could not get his breathing started in the preliminary humming exercises, as he felt that he was choking. He said he had just come from a dentist's appointment during which he had felt so much pain (unnecessarily inflicted, he thought) that he had wanted to scream, but couldn't. He finally began to relax and open his throat when a sudden knock on the studio door destroyed all progress. Dennis associated the knock with his childhood, when the landlord would storm upstairs and knock on his apartment door to protest his drumming. He said he has ever since been very frightened at hearing a knock on the door. Then he suddenly realized that he had been used by his parents as a foil against the landlord, and that he had felt guilty ever since for persisting with drum-ming, instead of submitting and stopping. The patient was urged to try to separate the past from the present, and to realize that the present situa-tion, one which he chose and had a right to, required his total effort and strength. He was able to continue after being encouraged to scream out the "ah" vowel on a descending five-tone scale.

The following week, Dennis executed the starting scale for the first time without losing or collapsing breath support. He then mentioned that he was having some difficulty in speaking during practice teaching. The music therapist asked him to pretend she was the class, while he demon-strated his teaching approach. He proceeded to show that he ran thoughts and phrases together without pause, gasping for shallow breaths throughout; he never completed a sentence or a breath or an idea; his presentation was frantic and disjointed, totally lacking the organizational development and technical means to make his basically good material comprehensible. As for breathing, he resisted incorporating what he had been taught and thus was hoarse and was straining his vocal chords. The music therapist remarked that his pattern indicated great constriction and fear, almost as if he had never known the feelings of safety or security. The patient picked this up immediately and related it to his mother's rejection of him at birth when she first viewed her unattractive infant son. He said she had screamed at seeing him, and he felt that he had always carried the memory of that scream in his ears. He believed it was the cause of his hypersensitivity to loud sounds. Dennis then asked for concrete help with his speaking difficulties. He wrote down three simple steps to follow, if possible, with major concentration for one whole day: (1) do not be afraid to pause; (2) empty the lungs, close the mouth and breathe through the nose after each pause; (3) speak only when supported by the breath using diaphragmatic control.

During the next session, the patient became aware that he must always sabotage success—that he had felt this urge grow stronger as his breathing improved and he became able to speak and sing without strain. The music therapist suggested this related to guilt, probably stemming from underlying hostility. The patient spoke of his hostility toward his rejecting sister and of his father's intense hostility toward him. The talk unnerved him and he became preoccupied. He suddenly realized he didn't *want* to hear the music therapist's instructions, and that he had never paid attention to his elders—as they were the enemies. The music therapist reaffirmed that she was on *his* side: he said he knew this and must learn to react more to the present and not be so ready to get trapped in the sewer drains of the past.

Two weeks later, Dennis started the session by saying he had become aware that much of his hostility toward females was pure imitation of his father's attitude. Work was then begun on the exercises. An unusual pattern soon became evident: in attacking notes, using either the hum or vowel sounds, both placement and tone production were finer at the end of the attack than at the onset. When this was pointed out, the patient said the same comment had been made by his clarinet and violin teachers. Together, the music therapist and the patient traced this tendency to his defensive, cautious, self-protective attitude—one of basic fearfulness and constriction. The patient then related it to the merry-go-round accident when he was nine and the emotional paralysis which had followed. He said he felt strongly that the tension points in his neck, throat, solar plexus and genital-anal area must be worked out in music therapy, and that breathing held the key to the problem. The music therapist urged the patient to go back to the time of trust and innocence *before* the merry-go-round accident; she assured him that she would never let him down or suddenly let go of her responsibility. The patient tried the humming scale again and was totally successful at the onset of attack all the way through! He said afterward that he had had to fight dizziness and anxiety every moment, as he had feared that the music therapist would *stop* playing the piano. From the time of this session, there was a marked decrease of hostility in this patient's behavior.

At the following session, Dennis said his throat was invariably tight when he taught or played drums. He knew this stemmed from hostility and anxiety and the desire to scream because of all the early objections to his playing drums. It was pointed out that the drums he chose had actually been the means of his salvation: he had clung to them despite enormously unpleasant circumstances; they had led him to New York where they now provided the income to underwrite his therapy and teacher-training; they were making possible his struggle to find himself, so that he need not become the victim his father was. *He need not become his father*! This discussion provided material which helped the patient, in psychotherapy, to resolve his ambivalent feelings about assuming the role of a teacher.

In fact, Dennis' case is altogether unusual because of the extraordinary amount of repressed material which surfaced in the music therapy situation, which was then referred back to the psychiatrist either by the music therapist or the patient himself. Also unusual in a music therapy setting were the incidences of abreaction and working through of repressed material. As may be inferred from the foregoing highlights, there were four facilitating factors: (1) the patient's acute aural sensitivity; (2) the direct and essential involvement in music therapy of the patient's foci of extreme tension; (3) the intimate connection of these tension points to repressed traumatic experiences; (4) the relationship of trust and confidence with the music therapist.

The progress made resulted primarily from the positive quality of this relationship and the fact that the music therapist understood the unconscious elements underlying the patient's behavior, such as his intense Oedipal strivings, passivity, castration anxieties, guilt reactions, and so on. As far as the patient was concerned, as he gained the courage to risk shattering his fancied fragile head and neck, he learned to breathe again— to exhale and inhale—to expand all the way and to contract all the way—to release tension and constriction — to *let go*. At the same time, he was learning to build up his chest wall, to stand well-poised and balanced, with feet firmly on the ground. As he learned to use breathing consciously as a part of his defense system, especially when confronted with challenges and difficulties, he began to be able to participate more actively and successfully in reality. This was accompanied by a marked reduction of psychosomatic symptoms—of headaches, choking, fatigue and gastrointestinal upsets. With growing self-confidence and control, he began to act more independently, and to exercise initiative and creativity. He was increasingly able to identify in the role of male authority figure, to find and give satisfaction whether as teacher, professional musician, son or friend and, eventually, as husband and father (Tyson, 1966).

3. *Maria*

A 39-year-old widow, Maria B., referred by a mental hygiene clinic, was suffering from a psychoneurosis characterized by marked ambivalence, depressive reactions and recourse to preoccupying fantasy. She presented herself as a fearful, inhibited woman, immobilized by lack of confidence and uncertainty about "going it alone." She said she had sought psychiatric treatment following her husband's death three years before, when her seven-year-old son had become extremely hostile and withdrawn out of a feeling of desertion, whereupon mother and son had begun to interact destructively. Maria was presently attending secretarial school and, in the meantime, had been encouraged by her psychiatrist to resume her former interest in the guitar (Tyson, 1966). The following rehabilitation objectives were indicated: encourage independence; provide self-gratification; stimulate creative expression; discourage perfectionism.

The early sessions revealed that, although the patient was definitely musical, her naturally good ear was blocked by extreme anxiety, and her instinctive feeling for the instrument was almost obliterated by clumsiness and stiffness arising from severe physical tension. She was terrified of making a mistake and, in general, was overconcerned with pleasing the music therapist. Without the sanction of the music therapist, she was unable to recognize her own abilities or accept the obvious progress she began to make. The only gratification she acknowledged was from singing—in a small, sweet voice—her favorite folk songs. She would become "rattled" when faced with new learning, and attributed this to her fear of new situations and tasks. She learned to cope more satisfactorily with this fear after repeatedly acting upon the suggestion that she set up an ultimate goal for herself (in music) and then smaller intermediate action goals, and that she look for improvement rather than perfection.

By the fifteenth session, despite steady progress in learning and applying chords, Maria continued to depreciate herself and her abilities. However, she seemed to be acquiring a little more realistic view of herself and her problems. She remarked that her son had become very distraught the week before, after reliving his father's death. When asked if she ever did likewise, she said she was the "strong one" among her family and friends; it was, therefore, a great relief and stabilizer to be able to come to the Center where she could be herself.

At the twenty-fifth session, Maria's strong perfectionistic tendencies again came to the fore. No matter how well she played (that is, smooth chord changes, executed swiftly, appropriately and in tempo), she always felt her performance was "terrible," "awful." The music therapist pointed out that she was unable to accept achievement because this would mean accepting responsibility, which she feared. With further discussion, the patient revealed her deep guilt feelings over her husband's death, as well as the death of her father and the miscarriage of her twin. She said she felt very frightened that her fleeting thoughts of death had eventuated in reality, and she felt omnipotently responsible. Maria subsequently reported her psychiatrist's confirmation that the fear of assuming responsibility was linked to the heretofore repressed guilt feelings.

The next sessions were cut short by the patient's increased unconscious resistance; she arrived each time about 25 minutes late. Despite this, her playing showed marked improvement; all at once, there was less tension, hesitancy and anxiety, and there seemed to be a partial unblocking of her aural perception.

At this point, Maria was completing secretarial training and preparing somewhat fearfully to look for work. She wanted a job at a college or university, so that she might eventually obtain a degree. When she complained that her difficulties with stenography and typing increased the harder she tried, she realized that the same mechanism applied to the guitar.

At the thirty-ninth session, there was no music whatsoever. Maria talked the entire time about her difficulties in finding a suitable job. She spoke of an emotional block which prevented her from functioning in a situation unless she could control every detail to the smallest degree. The music therapist suggested that the need to control a situation related to the need to control herself and the anger within her. After a pause, Maria agreed. Suddenly, she exploded in an outburst of rage: she was angry at her husband for dying and leaving her alone in such an unprotected position, angry at her brother who was born when she was three-and-a-half, and who became the focus of her parents' attention, angry at her parents for lavishing all their attention and efforts and love on the brother. She felt that her parents had ignored her ever since her brother's birth; no matter what she had tried to do, it never had seemed enough to please them. Maria said she had felt like a failure since she was three-and-a-half. After she regained her composure, she said she knew this must be the original anger, long-repressed, which led to the problems with her son after her husband's death.

There was little music during the sessions immediately following the outburst; rather, there was an outpouring of talk by the patient. She spoke of her frustrations and difficulties regarding her anger and job-finding efforts. She spoke at length about her guilt and fears as a result of the anger and, again, of how terribly frightened she was of the magical omnipotence of her thoughts. She spoke of the tension and compulsiveness and perfectionism which had caused her to lose several job opportunities. The music therapist offered guidance, support and reassurance, as needed, to which the patient eagerly responded. Gradually, there was a return to guitar-playing, and Maria was pleased to discover that she could now play by ear with relative ease. Shortly thereafter, she reported having passed a test for just the sort of job she had always dreamed of, and said it would not have been possible without the Center's help. As she succeeded at the job, she began to reach out to explore new interests and activities. One day, she spoke of her pride and happiness in the fact that her son was an outstanding child and student.

At the eighty-fifth session, the patient expressed the wish to discontinue music therapy, as there was a conflict with driving lessons (originally suggested by the music therapist) which she preferred at this time.

Maria's case provides another instance of repressed feelings and memories arising to the surface in the course of music therapy. The essential problem was the self-defeating effect of her neurotic defenses when confronted by normal job demands. The facilitating factors were: (1) The activity aspect of learning to play the guitar reflected in microcosm the same self-defeating effects of Maria's neurotic defenses; (2) The non-threatening character of the music therapy setting, wherein the fear of disastrous consequence of failure or self-revelation is minimized, helped to reduce restraint and loosen defensive safeguards; (3) The music therapist's awareness and effective use of the dynamics underlying the patient's positive transference aided the processes of identification and ego-incorporation (Tyson, 1966).

99911

4. *Jerry*

Jerry M. was eight and one-half years old when he was referred by a clinic for retarded children. The psychiatrist provided the following diagnostic information: mild multiple congenital anomalies; organic brain damage; borderline intelligence. The boy's characteristic behavior was described as insecure and fearful, with restlessness and low attention span. In addition to the child, both parents were being seen at the clinic periodically, to receive help in changing their overprotective and ineffectual ways. It was quickly observed during Jerry's first two sessions at the Center that the parents were overreacting to the clinic's suggestions: in their anxiety to be firmer, they literally pushed and incessantly threatened their son to achieve at a higher level. As a result of this constant pressure and criticism, Jerry was extremely overwrought and pathetically overconcerned about performing up to expectations.

During the first session, which the mother attended, she interrupted many times to remind the music therapist to be firm, as this was what the doctor had advised. At first, Jerry was so frightened that he could not enter the studio and, once in, would not sit down; he was so tense he could not unclench his fist at the piano keyboard, or loosen his grip on the xylophone stick. He moved clumsily and resisted physical activity. He spoke with difficulty and such poor articulation that it was almost impossible to understand him. He constantly asked if he was doing all right and, at every turn, looked beseechingly to his mother for approval. At the close of the session, the mother was informed by the director, in Jerry's presence, that hereafter the family would not be permitted to sit in on Jerry's sessions except at his own invitation (Tyson, 1966).

Both parents accompanied Jerry the second time. He could hardly wait to get on with the exploration of instruments and with playing the musical games which had been started the week before. Suddenly, the mother entered the studio and for fully five minutes insisted that he play the xylophone (which she had bought for him) just right. Jerry hesitatingly asked her to leave the room and finally, in no uncertain terms, ordered her to do so. He was soon enjoying himself thoroughly, clapping out rhythms and trying to mouth the words of simple songs. With encouragement, he was letting go, singing quite freely and loudly, when the father burst into the room and sternly admonished Jerry to "behave" and sing quietly. The music therapist assured the father that Jerry's noisiness was desirable at this point, and asked him to return to the waiting-room. The parents were so perturbed by the ensuing racket which emanated from the studio that the only way the session could continue undisturbed was for the director to bar their entrance by standing before the door throughout the balance of the session.

Thus, because Jerry presented such fearful, inhibited behavior, the initial approach was: (1) to establish a completely permissive and accepting atmosphere conducive to "free outflow" (over the parents' objections); (2) to abandon the parents' demands for fine co-ordination on the xylophone in favor of stimulating and channeling expressive and gross motoric responses; (3) to demonstrate to the patient (and, coincidentally, to the parents) the primacy of the therapist's relationship to him.

During the first five sessions, the music therapist sought a satisfactory means of communication, as Jerry did not respond to and, indeed, resisted with hostility, the nursery rhymes and folk tunes most children know and love. He clearly derived gratification from hammering at things in a very disorganized, haphazard and infantile manner, but little could be done to "harness" this propensity because of his extremely limited attention span. At the sixth session, the music therapist happened to play the Hebrew melody "Hagilah," and Jerry was instantly delighted. He was evidently familiar with the tune, having heard his father sing it many times. He began to move to the rhythm and to make up words to the melody. He sang about his brothers whom he said he hated; he sang about his dog Prince which he had loved and lost because his mother couldn't tolerate the mess it made in the house; he sang about his friend Joey and other friends at school, and about playing Cowboys and Indians with them; he sang about fighting with his brother; he sang about his Uncle Ira whom he loved. Along with this improvisation, Jerry was suddenly able to execute a one-two beat on the drum, and roll the plastic ball rhythmically while singing. Contact had at last been established!

The bongo drum was a particularly helpful instrument, strongly indicated by the extent of Jerry's bottled-up hostility and the intense frustration he experienced because of his inability to make himself understood. The effort to express himself was sometimes exhausting; when the words or names came out with difficulty, he would bang on the drum with venom. When he spoke of fighting with his brothers, he would pound upon the drum with unbelievable ferocity. Once he was filled with hostility throughout the session; he beat on the drum unmercifully and then pounded angrily on the piano and even the pedals, as if to destroy everything. Then he began to voice his dread and insecurity about going to camp, and his resentment about having been hospitalized for a minor operation.

By the eleventh session, the mother reported progress in that Jerry was memorizing words (of songs) for the first time. He was less hyperactive and distractible, more self-confident and was beginning to express himself more freely, clearly and spontaneously. Also, his schoolteacher had noticed that he was more cooperative and displayed more initiative in class. Mrs. M. was noticeably less tense. Jerry was quick to respond with affection and gratitude and cautiously began to take advantage of the support the Center provided. He frequently sought to prolong the sessions or, refusing to leave, would persist in shutting the door in his parent's face.

Musical progress was confined to Jerry's sense of rhythm, which was becoming more clearly defined; he had by now established a definite rhythmic pulse and had even caught fine distinctions such as syncopation; he also "conducted" with a baton with gusto and precision. However, he was unable to reproduce melodic lines.

Jerry often directed entire sessions to act out pent-up feelings symbolically, after which he would communicate the precipitating incident. He enjoyed imaginative play around the role of father, general or chief and clearly revealed his strong unconscious Oedipal strivings while playing "house" with the music therapist. He began to show a craving for people and frequently personified objects. One day, the plastic ball was a baby, while on another day it became three children at school whom he beat mercilessly.

In role-playing a naughty rabbit, he could not get himself to sing the part (admit to naughtiness) but agreed to play it on the drum; four sessions later he still had to deny misdeeds, but at the next session he gleefully sang "John the Rabbit" and enjoyed the naughtiness for the first time; three sessions later he asked to sing "Jerry the Rabbit" and it was frequently requested thereafter.

On the other hand, Jerry instantly took to the "fireman game," wherein he descended a ladder by playing the black notes one at a time from the top of the keyboard down. In this game, he always carried his father to safety but invariably slipped while carrying his mother and dropped her "by accident."

Jerry was obviously more restrained and inhibited when his mother was present. Mrs. M. tended to be judgmental and suspicious of her son's reactions, and quick to interpret his behavior as psychotic. She seemed unable to understand the nature of brain damage, or to accept assurances that her son would gradually outgrow some of his difficulties and much of his hyperactivity. She was frequently punitive and one day strapped him in the school lavatory after his teacher had complained of inattention.

The mother became extremely tense and Jerry correspondingly anxious when the teacher reported another problem at school, one involving difficulty in copying from the blackboard. The music therapist suggested that this might be a possible consequence of brain damage and thus a specific contributing factor to his learning difficulties; she urged the parent to consult with the clinic for further diagnostic work-up. As a result of this recommendation, the clinic suggested a preliminary eye examination before setting up special training procedures to remedy the difficulty in copying. The examination revealed, among other things, a partial paralysis of one eye that caused double vision. Additional testing confirmed the fact that Jerry's problem was rooted in organicity; he was subsequently transferred to a class for brain-damaged children.

By the twenty-sixth session, improvement was noted in muscular control and co-ordination, in lengthened attention span, in articulation and vocabulary, and in the use of sentences. In addition, Jerry was beginning to accept direction. Musical progress was noted in the growing ability to match tones and sing on pitch.

One day, Mrs. M. arrived in a very dispirited state. Evidently the clinic had re-tested Jerry and reported a lower IQ score than previously. The mother needed considerable reassurance that psychological development was more important at this time — that Jerry's behavior was much improved and that, as an adult, he would probably become absorbed in the normal population if only he could grow up with confidence. This very day, Jerry acted out a musical story about two brothers, one of whom smothered their mother because she was a nagging, vicious woman. Several sessions later, in play, in the role of his father, he again killed his mother.

Up until this time, as Jerry was not particularly musical and may even have been irritated by sounds, the sessions were primarily devoted to play therapy, utilizing music to dramatize daily occurrences along more or less stereotyped lines of current television programs. As noted, he eagerly looked forward to role-playing and derived obvious satisfaction from the release of pent-up emotions, the acting out of aggressive feelings and self-assertion within a dramatic framework. As he gradually became more interested in music and obtained greater pleasure from it, the sessions became more highly structured: generally 15 minutes at the piano, 15 minutes of singing, ending with 15 minutes of dramatic play.

By the sixty-fourth session, the patient displayed more initiative, maturity and self-confidence; he was now capable of conversing with continuity and focus; gross co-ordination continued to improve and new emphasis and progress were noted in fine muscle control; he began to enjoy physical contact which he previously could not tolerate; he appeared better organized and seemed to derive more satisfaction in life, although school was not one of these satisfactions. Musically, gains were made in voice pitch and word recall, in growing ability to anticipate notes and to sing short phrases rather than just end-rhymes.

At this point, Jerry confided that a serious problem had developed at school. His teacher was writing unfavorable reports to his mother, who would burst into tears upon reading them and then beat him. The reports complained of incomplete written assignments. Jerry showed the music therapist a large lump on the back of his head, the result of a bad report. He also shuddered violently at the sight of his teacher's handwriting, which he equated with the beatings. He pleaded for help.

The situation was discussed with the patient's psychiatrist, particularly the persistent use of threat and physical intimidation by both the mother and the teacher. The Center's director then conferred with the mother, pointing out that she was reacting immaturely to the teacher's criticism, as if she herself were the misbehaving student, and that her inability to act other than punitively stemmed from underlying rejection and distrust of her child. The mother reluctantly conceded that results to date strongly supported the diagnosis of brain damage, and she iterated the need to "control" herself. The ensuing discussions brought out the mother's basic agreement with the teacher's viewpoint, the manifest unfairness of punishing Jerry for difficulties he could not control, and the fact that trying to force miraculous results by intimidation was surely leading to the creation of serious emotional problems.

Mrs. M. suddenly blurted out that she had always fought the idea of brain damage because she felt responsible; she fell off a ladder the day before giving birth to Jerry. She could not accept the explanation that the baby was completely formed in utero by then. She said she had felt "hurt" ever since Jerry was born and realized that she has been wearing herself out by not accepting reality. She also said that some of her tenseness was a reaction against Jerry's "suffering"; however, she readily saw that he was far more disturbed because of her tension and rejection than because of his brain damage. This discussion marked a turning-point in the case.

As Mrs. M.'s defensiveness and resistance crumbled, she began to pick up cues from the behavior of Jerry's music therapist and the Center's director. Each demonstrated wholehearted, unconditional acceptance of Jerry for what he was; each was his ally who granted credence to his point of view and actively responded to his pleas for help; each emphasized the importance of emotional satisfaction and maturation over academic achievement. Mrs. M. was persuaded to experiment by forcing herself to ignore Jerry's school record, at first for a week, and then for ever-lengthening periods. Positive changes soon followed: he became more relaxed, more self-confident, more reasonable; he dropped many infan-tilisms; there was noticeable further improvement in attention span, concentration, articulation, speech content and motor co-ordination; he evinced more contact, warmth, and movement toward trust and in-volvement; he became more interested in music and in physical activity; his school adjustment improved markedly although his grades remained poor. An important development during this last phase was the begin-ning of oral play by way of sucking, touching, singing and "parties" during which Jerry suddenly began to eat sweets with great relish, almost voraciously. This was significant because of a history of force-feeding.

At the Center's suggestion, Mrs. M. decreased the heavy schedule of extracurricular activities and specific therapies that her unrealistic hopes had foisted on Jerry; she began to join him in outdoor activities such as bicycle riding, skating, rowing boats, and for the first time, they enjoyed simple pleasures together. It was a happy day for all when a relaxed Mrs. M. announced that there just didn't seem to be the need or the time to continue making the long weekly trip to the Center—and one glance at relaxed, happy Jerry showed that this was so.

The unusual element in this case was the exceptional involvement of the parents, especially the mother. Out of her refusal to accept her son's limitations and her drive to perfect him, she saw to it that this relatively unmusical retarded child was referred for music therapy. Her actions were not only the result of a denial of subconscious guilt—they reflected, as well, the family's normal social values and cultural drives. These had combined to form for Jerry a somewhat sophisticated and critical veneer over a virtually undeveloped central core where little *real* response or involvement had ever been generated.

Jerry's adjustment and progress in the music therapy setting was unde-niably good, and his level of interpersonal response, undeniably high. His positive experiences and behavior at the Center helped bring into focus the mother's pivotal role in relation to his poor adjustment and response at school. When later developments obviously implicated the mother, a direct confrontation brought to the surface hitherto repressed or withheld material which held the key to a more constructive modus vivendi for mother and child. The facilitating factor was the relationship of trust and confidence which was established between Jerry and his music therapist, and which permitted the revelation of his deepest fear and problems.

Music itself was used as a medium to elicit response and communica-tion, to permit the safe and uninhibited release of aggressive and hostile feelings, to stimulate imagery and speech, to initiate and regulate motor activity. Structure was introduced and paced at the level of the patient's capacity (Tyson, 1966).

5. *Kathy*

The following study, extremely condensed, is from a case of long-term individual music therapy with a chronic schizophrenic woman. Although the patient worked with a number of the Center's music therapists over the years, the description focuses almost exclusively on the conduct of sessions and relationship with the author as therapist; it also reveals the intimate connection between music and early traumatic experiences in the life of this patient (Tyson, 1979).

> Kathy, at age twenty-seven, was referred to CARC for piano study. Her psychiatrist gave the diagnosis: pseudoneurotic schizophrenia. Characteristic behavior patterns included: fear of being attacked; suspiciousness; depression; immobilization; repressed, impotent rage followed by withdrawal into fantasy. The following rehabilitation objectives were given: improve socialization and interpersonal communication; build self-esteem; strengthen reality contact; increase verbalization; induce socially-acceptable behavior; provide outlet for aggression and tension; encourage independence; stimulate creative expression.

This patient had grown up in a highly-disturbed poverty-stricken family; the parents were unaware of their destructive influence upon their children. As a child, she had withdrawn from life and from those around her. Each day had been a struggle in a losing battle to define herself, to feel some sense of value and to simply survive. From age seventeen, there were twenty hospitalizations in city and state mental institutions, and a myriad of treatments endured with little result.

During her first contacts at the Center, Kathy was extremely frightened, tense and distractible. She could not look at one directly or speak except by mumbling and leaving each thought or sentence unfinished. She would sit with downcast head, nervously twisting and untwisting her long, thin fingers and occasionally whisper: "Don't know what I am," or "Feel all dried up."

Frequently, she would dart away to be found hours later hidden under the lowest shelf or in the most inaccessible corner of a closet. In general, she was overwhelmed by frustration and by feelings of futility and unworthiness; she was preoccupied with thoughts of death; she denied angry feelings and resented any manifestation or interpretation of illness, to which she responded with shame and humiliation.

The opportunity to study music again (she had had four years of study in childhood) appeared to be intensely important to Kathy. She expressed the conviction that much of her "supposed" illness showed itself in relation to the piano and that, if everything were right with her and the piano, somehow her life could be straightened out. She feared we would not accept the fact that she was unable to finish a piece, and could only play "loud"—she liked to bang hard on the keyboard.

During the initial sessions, the patient revealed that she felt trapped, helpless and powerless in a hostile, dark and cold world; she felt she would know peace only when she could choke her mother the way her mother had once choked her; she frequently improvised songs about killing her mother and sister; she became aware of the hatred within her

and of how it made her feel ugly, evil, wretched and guilty; she felt unable
to cope with unbearable or unpleasant feelings or situations except by
wanting to obliterate them or by running away or using magical thinking.
She begged for help to find solutions for her feelings of helplessness and
unreality.

Exceptional rapport developed almost at once between Kathy and her
music therapist. She felt trust and love and, for the first time in many
years, said she felt she *must* struggle to speak and to communicate, as it
would now be safer than silence. Psychological evaluation during a prior
hospitalization had revealed that her early childhood was experienced as
intensely destructive, rejecting, depriving and quarrelsome. The family
setting was likened to "a war of animals." Her longing for closeness was
countered by fear of victimization, censure and moral recrimination from
a harsh, cruel mother figure whom the patient had internalized and was
also desperately struggling to cast out. In childhood, she had felt so
hopeless about being understood or having her needs taken care of that
she had stopped talking for many years. This had led to an assumption of
stupidity and mental retardation by her family and the school system, to
which the patient now stubbornly clung. She also bore what she felt to be
an indelible imprint at the very core of her psyche that she was born a
"rotten, evil, bad seed," and that she, herself, had caused all the pain and
suffering she had endured.

"When I was very young, I didn't grow up with my sister or my brothers. I
was placed in children's shelters most of the time with my next oldest brother.
I didn't grow up with one of my brothers either, 'cause my mother had him
put in reform school.

Part of the time, my father was in prison, and part of the time, my parents
were separated. Part of the time, my mother was in the hospital because she
swallowed iodine.

When we were living at home, everybody fought and hated everybody
else. My mother used to tell everybody how bad my father was. . . she used to
pick on him a lot. He was also blind. Then he'd start banging his head against
the wall, saying how he wished he was dead."

Kathy perceived her psychiatrist as malicious and rejecting; she distrusted him and regarded him as an enemy. She felt she could not and
would not communicate with him. She "hated" his insistence that she
was ill—that her anger was her problem and that, if she could recognize it,
her depressions would be relieved. She felt it necessary to put on a front
of perfection, wellness, strength and capability when she saw him, as she
so feared he might send her back to the hospital. On the other hand, she
feared disappointing him.

A lifetime of rejection led to Kathy's response of massive self-rejection,
which included the *music* which she so desperately wished to pursue, but
was so totally unable to approach. Her innate high musicality and considerable talent were prevented from developing by her guilt feelings and
self-rejecting tendency. She felt guilty at the thought of having talent. She
didn't finish pieces because that would be "good" and she fought any
possibility of good in herself. If she were to complete or perfect a piece, it
would make her so fear the piano that she would have to stop playing.

Kathy's early childhood was experienced as destructive, depriving and quarrelsome. The family setting was likened to a war of animals. Parental figures and siblings are seen as clashing, attacking, out to kill each other, and Kathy was in between. Severely traumatized, she had recoiled from all contact into a self-protective seclusiveness.

Her life was full of terror. Kathy was brought up in terror and she lived in terror of everyone and everything. In her only realistic self-portrait, terror is plainly evident in her facial expression and in the dissociation from her body and bodily feelings. Her helplessness is evident through the absence of hands.

"When I first came to the Center, all I could do was bang
and bang and bang and bang. I was banging all the hurt
and the anger. But even after I was finally able to
express something delicate in the music I first had to start
with banging."

Kathy felt trapped, helpless and powerless in a hostile, dark and cold
world. Frequently, she would dart away to be found hours later under
the lowest shelf or in the most inaccessible corner of a closet. She was
overwhelmed by frustration, feelings of futility and unworthiness. She
reacted with shame and humiliation to any interpretation of illness.

Whenever Kathy's fingers became rigidly arched back away
from the keys we understood that she was hallucinating.
The "voices" were telling her to stop playing, to cut off her
hands, to set fire to the piano, to kill herself.

Because of massive self-rejection, the music which she so desperately
wished to pursue she was totally unable to approach.

"I feel that so much of my illness shows itself in relation
to the piano, and I'm convinced that if everything were right
with me and the piano somehow, everything would fall in
place in my life."

"I hear the music that I love. Its beauty creates a kind of twisting
and tearing inside of me.
For I cannot feel such intense love without memories of past hurts
and sorrows."

Music alone does not change behavior. Behavioral changes take place in the context of the relationship. When Kathy's loving and tender feelings grew towards the music therapist, she expressed the need to bite and mouth her fingertips. As this patient was split over an intense inner struggle to cast out the internalized destructive mother figure, the music therapist decided to go along with Kathy's need to incorporate her orally.

This repeated process always resulted in Kathy's intense delight and produced noticeable change. For the first time in her life she permitted physical closeness and affectionate intimacy.

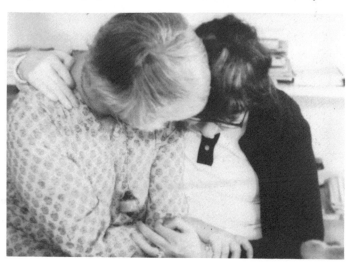

"Through attending the Center, I learned to trust, I learned self-respect, and I learned to love."

She experienced feelings of dread and discomfort in relation to practicing, and she was fearful of being hit or attacked from behind.

"When I was about nine, my mother made me practice the piano and play only what the piano teacher had given me and nothing more. I was not allowed to play my own pieces or my own arrangements. My mother would stand by and hold a yard-stick. If I disobeyed, she would strike me, sometimes missing and leaving dents on the piano keys from the force. My mother had gone to a tea-leaf reader, and was told that her daughter would be a concert pianist.

One day, I was practicing—my mother directing and standing by, as usual. Suddenly, I felt very tired and wanted to stop. My mother refused to let me. I started to get up and move away from the piano. My mother grabbed me from behind—first my shoulders and then my neck. She threatened me and said that if I didn't practice she would kill me. She was yelling and wild. At that moment, my father came through the door and tried to separate us. He could not, at first, and kept striking my mother until she let go. It was after this that I began to sleep with a knife to protect myself."

At the start of music therapy, Kathy revealed that she handled hurt and pain by forcing herself to become "unreal." Her attention span was very limited and, once, after a moment of success in ear-training, she spoke of her reluctance to abandon the mist on her concentration, because the concentration which would clarify musical problems might also sharpen the clarity of painful life problems. Initially, the patient could only bang on the keyboard. More tender feelings were too painful to express as they were associated with feeling "real." Her poem reveals the difficulty:

"I hear the music that I love
Its beauty creates a kind of
twisting and tearing inside of me.

For I cannot feel such intense love
without memories of past hurts and sorrows."

Thus it was that the possibility of further music study depended upon the prior resolution of severe psychological problems. Weekly sessions revolved at first about two functions: (1) To establish and maintain communication by providing primitive gratification at the oral level—at each session, food was shared which the therapist provided, while both sat cross-legged on the floor before an imaginary camp-fire; (2) To explore and identify evidences of ability and musicality at the piano keyboard, at every opportunity.

With the long-range view of serving rehabilitation objectives, the over-all approach aimed to: (1) Provide a sense of security to the "inner child" in the patient, in a symbolic way; (2) Provide a safe atmosphere and channels for the release of repressed hostility; (3) Encourage the verbal expression of angry or negative feelings; (4) Provide the patient with an ally and a model for positive identification; (5) Provide unshakable belief that she was not basically bad, and that her rights and needs must no longer be denied; (6) Help her perceive a causal relationship between events and her behavior; (7) Stress the importance of her doctor's role to her survival and safety, to clarify her resistance to him, and to help her to communicate with him.

Shortly after starting music therapy, Kathy came to the Center late one Friday evening, just at closing time. She was shaken and trembling, after having tried unsuccessfully to reach her doctor. She had strong feelings of being pushed around and of being trapped, and she feared she might kill someone. However, she insisted that she, Kathy, was not angry—it was *Gail!* In casting about for a way to help her, the music therapist took as a cue her banging predilection on the keyboard and said: "All right, then, let's kill—on the piano!" Over and over, Kathy pounded through a favorite short section of the Beethoven "Emperor" Concerto. She was urged on: "Kill! Kill! Break the piano! Who do you want to kill?" *"Mother!"* "Kill! Kill! Harder! etc." After almost an hour of mounting attack of this kind, the patient obtained release. She requested immediate reassurance that the therapist cared for her.

For many months thereafter, Kathy had pounding sessions on Friday nights, which helped her to breathe and obtain release. When it was suggested that withheld anger was the cause, the patient finally said that was her doctor's view. Discussions were directed toward her frequent violent headaches after seeing her mother or older sister. It was pointed out that since her mother's recent visit, she had permitted Gail to swamp her and take over, and that this was unnecessary—Kathy can be *nice* and angry at the same time. "You mean Gail is my anger?" Kathy said that she could only let go on the piano; that she *had* to come to the Center on Fridays to pound, otherwise she would not feel safe over the week-end.

At a subsequent pounding session, the patient could not "kill her mother" directly on the piano; she asked that it be self-inflicted pain. First, the music therapist exhorted her to see how much pain Kathy could inflict, then how much Gail could, then how much both together could. The latter suggestion was most gratifying, although the patient had great difficulty remembering to join Kathy and Gail. Finally, she repeated the same Beethoven passage to the point of exhaustion, at times in a state close to frenzy. She was markedly relieved and relaxed at the end and, during the following week, was able to read and concentrate on work for the first time in many years.

After another savage Kathy/Gail pounding session shortly thereafter, the patient said she hated her doctor for saying she was angry all the time. She insisted she wasn't!

At the next pounding session, the Beethoven phrase was again shared by Kathy/Gail. For the first time, the therapist assured the patient that she (who was capable of all the varieties of emotion) was infinitely stronger than Gail (who only represented the single emotion of anger). The patient said she could visualize Gail playing, but not Kathy; she needed to think of something "human." The music therapist suggested herself walking hand-in-hand with Kathy, down a road. She agreed and played out her part with strength, tenderness and beauty, totally vanquishing Gail.

The following week, for the first time, the patient asked: "Shall we see how angry *Kathy* is?" She was extremely fearful but, with much encouragement and the support of two-against-one, finally sent Gail scurrying away forever. At this point, the patient telephoned her music therapist at least once daily to ask: "Do you still love me?" She needed endless reassurance that she was not bad, that it was all right for Kathy to be angry and that she was still loved.

About one month later, the patient said she felt she was perilously hanging onto the piano, but could only do so blindly—if she were to let go and fall, it would mean having to stop playing forever. Although she asked to drop piano for guitar, she was really requesting assurance that she would *never* be permitted to drop piano. She asked: "Why?" And waited to hear it said that it was very deeply important to her life, and that her very existence, rights, needs and desires must no longer be denied. The assurance she sought seemed almost a matter of life and death—of her very sanity. Shortly thereafter, the music therapist received the following note: "I loved you when you said you wouldn't let me stop. I feel there is a chance for things to be all right, and safer, somehow. It's the most security I've ever had in my life. Actually, the *only* security." Later, it was possible to relate the feeling that she would soon have to stop playing to symbolic suicide.

What should a music therapist do when faced with a patient's new and unusual behavior pattern? In this case, Kathy had never known, and could not permit, physical closeness or affectionate intimacy. As her loving and tender feelings grew toward the music therapist—the first she had ever experienced—she expressed the need to bite and mouth the therapist's fingertips. The primary psychiatrist was out-of-town at this time. The therapist searched for the clue in one hospital's diagnostic evaluation, which said that this patient was split over an intense inner struggle to cast out the internalized destructive mother figure. She decided to go along with Kathy's need to incorporate her through the mouth, by actually putting both hands into the patient's mouth and pretending to go in all the way until she said she could feel the therapist inside. This took place always to Kathy's intense delight and produced a new response. The patient said she now felt able to contemplate the possibility of long-range goals, although she was far from able to do anything about them as yet.

Kathy gradually began to accept that she had been born into an irrational atmosphere and that she had responded in kind, in ways that had helped her to survive. She tied in her extreme fearfulness at the piano with its extreme importance to her, and with her feeling of punishment if she pursued it. She was constantly provocative and testing. She fought fiercely against accepting her positive attributes. Also, she grew increasingly unable to put herself into a numb state—to become "unreal"—in order to escape pain and loneliness.

By the second year of music therapy, there were notable gains in the patient's spontaneity, outgoingness and verbalization. The outlines of her body and hands had become less rigid and tense. She felt for the first time that it was *she* producing music at the piano, *she* pressing down the keys, not someone else. She began to exchange some "hate" music (Bizet, de Falla) for a more varied repertoire. When by herself, she played with tenderness and beauty for longer periods at a time.

Kathy frequently put into writing what she found to difficult to verbalize. In the fourth year, she wrote this note:

"Most of the time when I play the piano it's for short periods—maybe fifteen minutes at the most. When I play for a longer period it's as though I was in a dream-like state and someone else is playing—not me. It sounds good. Then I have to stop. When I stop I feel very depressed — and hopeless and like wanting real bad either to die or lose consciousness. My music therapist asked if anyone ever *made* me stop. I said no. (My therapist said she didn't think I want to stop.) I said that when I'm really studying a piece and I've got it *almost* completed, I also have this hopeless and depressed feeling—and then I wouldn't touch or go near a piano for months or years. I tried to remember *when* I had last finished a piece of music.

Then I remembered Ellen. I met her in High School. She lived up my block. We were both pathetically lonely and friendless and although we didn't speak very much, we spent a good deal of time together. My mother didn't want me to see her anymore. (The reason she gave was that Ellen's father had committed suicide.) My mother said that if I didn't stop seeing her, she wouldn't buy me a winter coat. I said I'd do without the coat — and I wore my brother's jacket. Then she threatened to stop my music lessons, so I said I wouldn't see Ellen anymore. I felt guilty about making that decision—that it was weak of me to have made such a choice and that I betrayed my friend. Anyway, after that was when I couldn't finish a piece anymore."

After reading the note, Kathy's guilt regarding Ellen was discussed at length, as well as her rage at her mother for blackmailing her in such fashion. The therapist suggested that she need never leave music unfinished again. The next day, the patient came to the Center and played Grieg's "Wedding Day" all the way through, twice, for the first time. She was elated, euphoric and radiant—for the first time!

By the end of the fourth year, there were more frequent periods of being "real," during which the patient was able to communicate more freely, directly and with high intelligence. After each session, Kathy began to hug the music therapist—gingerly and timidly at first, but then with more confidence; the closer and tighter she could hug, the more "real" she would feel. Shyly, and with many giggles, she indicated that her breasts were growing larger. She showed more interest and care in grooming and in dressing attractively. She was trying more, and acting more to protect herself. Her body continued to soften and grow more feminine.

One of Kathy's severest problems, when repressing fierce anger, was the uncontrollable desire to bite, burn or cut herself. We did not learn of this for several years, as she had confined the action to her stomach and chest. Gradually, the scratches and gashes appeared on her arms and legs and, very often, welled open before one's eyes. It was a frightening experience for anyone to witness. We held the patient to her doctor's interpretation that each such action was an attempt to solve a more painful reality problem by inflicting physical pain which was easier for her to bear. And we insisted that she was capable of better solutions.

It was not until the fifth year that the patient revealed to anyone that she cuts because "they" tell her to—"they" being voices (loud, whispering female voices). The voices tell her in cold, bitter tones that she's bad; they tell her to bite and cut off or burn her hair, to get a gun, to put her hand in the stove flame, to stiffen her hands particularly when she is at the piano. She had never told this to anyone before because she had feared it would mean re-hospitalization. At this time, she also divulged her inability to listen to her beloved record collection — particularly Beethoven and Rachmaninoff—when alone at home; another person always had to be present to listen, as she felt she was not worth spending the electricity on.

The voices had started the year after High School, when she was going to night school preparatory to entering evening college. Her mother had belittled, criticized and ridiculed her strivings for higher education to such an extent that, when Kathy finally received a letter of acceptance from a city university, she tore it up, feeling certain that it must be an error. This was the time that Gail was born. The voices thereafter interfered with concentration on a job or with music or with anything she wanted to do. Her music therapist insisted she need not do what hateful, destructive forces desire. She can answer back. She can listen to voices which want to help and care about her. She asked for additional help, and arrangements were made with another staff member to "chase the voices away." The process consisted of repeated affirmation of our belief in her rights, capabilities and inherent goodness.

The voices began to diminish as Kathy became increasingly able to express angry feelings verbally and appropriately. Constant iteration of her mother's irrationality and blind egocentricity, and naming her mother's treatment as brutally unjust and unfair helped this patient, as did our giving voice to her negative feelings. Reactions to her were never "pulled"; platitudes or palliatives were never employed. Only deep honesty offered her anything, and facing and naming together the depths of despair and loneliness, of hopelessness and injustice and, finally, of love.

As with many other patients who have been referred to CARC, Kathy brought with her the one key that could be employed non-verbally to unlock her inner emotional world: her love of music. Music served as the lifeline to her survival and transformation, not only because it was so intensely meaningful to her, but because it was the only area in life in which she directly expressed any feeling at all. Her need to bang on the keyboard was accepted by the music therapist as symbolic communication, and Kathy was helped to safely give vent to fiercely repressed feelings of terror, rage and pain in this manner. Gradually, it became possible for more tender feelings to be expressed through music. As her expressive capabilities increased, so did her contact with reality. Music therapy enabled this patient to begin to integrate her ego, to move out of her inner world, to relate to others and take her place in the real world to an extent never before possible.

Music
and the Primary Relationship

There are many cases, similar to Kathy's, in which music plays a major facilitating role in establishing communication. Frequently, music-related events are uncovered in connection with repressed traumatic experiences. Because such a high proportion of these patients are schizophrenic, many questions recur: Why are we able to help the schizophrenic patient? What is the significance of the non-verbal aspect? Why do we spend so much time explaining the nature of resistance to patients in analytic treatment? Why are we able to help the "silent" or strongly independent patients, who so frequently fail in analytically-oriented therapy? What is the nature of a healing relationship? Where does music fit in?

Schizophrenia is considered to be a disorganization of the ego system (Hudson, 1973). According to Arieti (1967), it is a disorganization of the intrapsychic self system, causing the person to function at a more primitive level involving primary process and paleologic thinking. The impairment of cognitive functions which occurs in schizophrenia includes communicative function by means of language — the modus vivendi of most psychotherapy. How, then, can therapy proceed?

A viewpoint with implications for music therapy is provided by Balint (1968); it is briefly summarized in the following paragraphs. Balint describes the more primitive level of ego integration as the area of the "basic fault": its prevalent structure is an exclusively two-person relationship, more primitive than that obtaining between adults. The basic fault occurs at the point of childhood trauma; it results from the "lack of fit" between the child and his environment, which is attributed to mismanagement during the early formative periods by adults, particularly the mother. The level of mental processes as they appear in the therapeutic situation may be characterized as "pre-Oedipal" or "pre-genital" or "pre-verbal." At this level, the "child in the patient" is an "infant" who cannot speak the language of adults, and cannot bridge the gulf between himself and adults on his own.

The task of analytic therapy is to assist the patient to re-adapt the methods s/he developed to deal with the original trauma. If the trauma struck at a point beyond the Oedipal area, a considerable regression may be necessary so that the trauma can be re-lived. However, at the level of the basic fault, the true ego or self is so weak and immature that it cannot be expected to emerge unless a transitional positive "fit" is established between the individual and the demands of reality, which overpower him. "This very delicate piece of work, consisting of nursing, protecting, mediating, looking after, etc., is usually called 'management', which is an additional, or perhaps even more fundamental, task of analytical therapy at this level than those better known, such as sympathetic listening, understanding, and interpreting." The analyst's decision to gratify the patient's regressive urges and to accept positively the accompanying acting-out, is prompted by the unbearable frustrations and limitations inherent in the normal analytic situation which the patient is unable to tolerate.

Freud's writings did not deal at any length with the problems of therapeutic regression — only of defensive or pathogenic regression. Balint identifies beneficial regression with the concept of "new beginning," which means going back to a point before the faulty development started. All new beginnings take place in the transference, i.e., in an object relationship; they lead to a changed relationship in the patient's objects of love and hate, with subsequent diminution of anxiety, change in the ego and improved, more adaptive ways of coping.

The aim of the analyst is to establish an object relationship similar in structure to the primary relationship. S/he *becomes*, in effect, the environment, conducive to new beginning, which resembles that of *primary substances* or objects: s/he must be indestructible; s/he must be there and consent to be used much as the air the patient breathes or the water s/he swims in; s/he must not resist or cause irritation or friction; s/he must accept and carry the patient for awhile; s/he must allow the patient to co-exist in a kind of "harmonious, interpenetrating mix-up." The involvement of the analyst does not so much require action, as providing the conditions — unfettered time, space and understanding — in which events can take place internally, in the patient's mind. Incidentally, the role of primary object does not depend upon a female figure; a male analyst can fulfill the role, as well.

Traditional procedures of interpretation depend upon language, intellectual understanding and "insight"—all intrapersonal responses which do not necessarily involve another human being. In contrast, "object relationship" implies an interaction between at least two people, which may be created and maintained by nonverbal means. The result is a "feeling," which is symbolically expressed by some sort of physical contact such as touching—a basic constituent of the primary relationship.

The new beginning also includes "regression aimed at recognition," which encourages and respects the patient's internal life and individuality. A benign regression depends upon the ability of the analyst to reduce the gap of inequality and omnipotence between himself and the patient— to remain more ordinary in the patient's eyes, while at the same time maintaining the necessary amount of distance. Under these circumstances, the patient has the chance to discover, experience and experiment with new forms of object relationship, which can lead to inactivating or healing of the basic fault.

"The technical problem is how to offer 'something' to the patient which might function as a primary object, or at any rate as a suitable substitute for it ... on to which he can project his primary love. The aim is that the patient should be able to find himself, to accept himself, and to get on with himself, knowing all the time that there is a scar in himself, his basic fault, which cannot be analyzed out of existence; moreover, he must be allowed to discover *his* way to the world of objects ... If this can be done, the patient will not feel that the objects impinge on, and oppress, him." New patterns of relationship will emerge, less defensive and rigid, and more flexible, than heretofore, and they represent a significant step toward a better integration of the ego.

The implications of Balint's viewpoint for music therapy are clear if one substitutes "music therapist" for "analyst" and "music therapy" for "analytic therapy" in the foregoing paragraphs. Thus, the two-person relationship is fundamental to progress in music therapy when working with the regressed borderline or schizophrenic patient. The essential non-verbal means of interaction is provided by the musical activity, through which the acting-out is expressed. The "management" role of the music therapist is directed toward establishing a benign relationship which does not oppress the patient *musically*. That is why pleasurable and expressive aspects take precedence over technical musical requirements, especially during the initial phase of the relationship. "Recognition" is similarly obtained—by accepting the patient's musical desires or interest, and by helping him to find an expressive outlet as quickly as possible through his particular musical strengths or talent. The possibility of a shared mutual experience becomes realizable as both patient and music therapist share the love of music. Conversely, the patient must never have the feeling of pressure or superiority from the music therapist. This is particularly important with the regressed patient, who is prone to de-velop relationships of inequality, thereby further perpetuating his tendency to regression. Premature musical interpretations (although ob-jectively realistic) are perceived by the patient as hurtful, hostile or unjus-tified demands from which he must recoil. The needed margin of distance is derived from the distance which exists between the emotional experi-ence and the music that arouses this experience (von Lange, 1901). Music can "recall and paraphrase feelings, but it never arouses them directly" (Noy, 1967). The "something" to offer the patient as a substitute for a primary object is *music itself*, upon which he (and this has very often been true for the music therapist, as well) can project his primary love. And, in the transitional phase, it is the musical instrument—the guitar, the violin, the horn, the piano keyboard—which he touches and holds as symbol of feelingful relationship.

The meaning of music therapy could not be more finely expressed than by this note from a patient at Creative Arts Rehabilitation Center:

"In music therapy, the music therapist, by the very nature of musical accom-paniment, makes a profound psychological statement to the patient. He says: 'With this musical experience I will journey with you from the beginning of the piece (your struggle) to the end (transformation). I will go with you through anxiety, rhythm difficulties, fantasies, whether you finish or not. I will listen to you speak, even musically.' The good therapist becomes aware of this statement and when warranted becomes a guide, brother, sister, the good friend. There is the basic reality of patient and therapist coming to-gether, one human to another.

With accompaniment assured, the patient can explore strengths and weaknesses, realize his or her own potentials, and define problems. A patient even may become, in a monumental step toward maturity, *responsible* for his or her course. This reality also may occur in a highly structured session as long as the structure is always realized by the patient to be directed toward his growth, stability and self-discipline — as long as the demand aims at the patient's eventual responsibility and individuation."

Thus music, the language of the emotions, projects its own distinctive reality; it produces a realm—temporal and tonal—which is once-removed from life itself. Within this realm, music the art serves mankind's expressive, creative and aesthetic needs.

However, music alone cannot resolve emotional incapacity. Through music therapy, the regressed patient who is musically disposed is afforded uniquely favorable opportunities for experience and growth, for being and becoming, not only in relation to music, but to the music therapist and to himself as well.

References

Ainlay, G. W. "The Place of Music in Military Hospitals." In Schullian, D. M. and Schoen, M. (Eds.), MUSIC AND MEDICINE. Pp. 322–351. New York: Henry Schuman, Inc., 1948.

Altshuler, I. M. "Four Years' Experience with Music as a Therapeutic Agent at the Eloise Hospital." Pp. 792–794. AM. J. PSYCH. (100), May, 1944.

—— "A Psychiatrist's Experiences with Music as a Therapeutic Agent." In Schullian, D. M. and Schoen, M. (Eds.), MUSIC AND MEDICINE. Pp. 266–281. New York: Henry Schuman, Inc., 1948.

—— "Music Potentiating Drugs." In Gaston, E. T. (Ed.), MUSIC THERAPY 1955. Pp. 120–126. Lawrence, Kans.: National Association for Music Therapy, Inc., 1956.

—— and Shebesta, B. H. "Music (alone or with hydrotherapy): Aid in Management of the Psychotic Patient." Pp. 179–183. J. NERV. & MENT. DIS. (94), August, 1941.

Apel, W. (Ed.) "Music Therapy." HARVARD DICTIONARY OF MUSIC, 2nd ED. Cambridge, Mass.: The Belknap Press of Harvard University Press, 1969.

Arieti, S. THE INTRAPSYCHIC SELF. New York: Basic Books, 1967.

Balint, M. THE BASIC FAULT. London: Tavistock Publications, 1968.

Bernstein, L. THE UNANSWERED QUESTION. Cambridge, Mass.: Harvard Univ., 1975.

Black, B. J. (Ed.) GUIDES TO PSYCHIATRIC REHABILITATION. New York: Altro Health and Rehabilitation Services, 1963.

Blackwell, E. and Neal, G. A. "Music in Mental Hospitals." Pp. 243–246. OCCUP. THER. & REHABIL. (25), December, 1946.

Boenheim, C. "The Importance of Creativity in Contemporary Psychotherapy." JOURNAL OF MUSIC THERAPY, vol. IV, no. 1. Pp. 3–6. March, 1967.

—— "The Position of Music and Art Therapy in Contemporary Psychotherapy." JOURNAL OF MUSIC THERAPY, vol. V, no. 3. Pp. 85–87. September, 1968.

Bonny, H. L. and Pahnke, W. N. "The Use of Music in Psychedelic (LSD) Psychotherapy." JOURNAL OF MUSIC THERAPY, vol. IX, no. 2. Pp. 64–83. Summer, 1972.

—— and Savary, L. M. MUSIC AND YOUR MIND: LISTENING WITH A NEW CONSCIOUSNESS. New York: Harper & Row, 1973.

Boxberger, R. "Historical Bases for the Use of Music in Therapy." Pp. 125–166. In Schneider, E. H. (Ed.), MUSIC THERAPY 1961. Lawrence, Kansas: National Association for Music Therapy, Inc., 1962.

Branch, C. H. "Psychiatry Re-enters the Community." MENTAL HYGIENE (48). Pp. 343–350. 1964.

Braswell, C. "Psychiatric Music Therapy: A Review of the Profession." MUSIC THERAPY 1961. Pp. 53–64. Lawrence, Kans.: National Association for Music Therapy, Inc., 1962.

Carapetyan, A. "Music and Medicine in the Renaissance and in the 17th and 18th Centuries." In Schullian, D. M. and Schoen, M. (Eds.), MUSIC AND MEDICINE. Pp. 117–157. New York: Henry Schuman, Inc., 1948.

Clausen, J. A. SOCIOLOGY AND THE FIELD OF MENTAL HEALTH. New York: Russell Sage Foundation, 1956.

Connor, F. P., EDUCATION OF HOMEBOUND OR HOSPITALIZED CHILDREN, Bureau of Publications, Teachers College, Columbia University, New York: 1964.

Coriat, I. H. "Some Aspects of Psychoanalytic Interpretation of Music." PSYCHOANALYTIC REVIEW (32), Pp. 408–418, October, 1945.

Daly, D. D. and Barry, M. J., Jr. "Musicogenic Epilepsy: Report of Three Cases." Pp. 399–408. PSYCHOSOMATIC MEDICINE (19), 1957.

Deutsch, A. THE MENTALLY ILL IN AMERICA (2nd ed.) New York: Columbia University Press, 1949.

Diserens, C. M. "Reactions to Musical Stimuli." PSYCH. BULL., 1922.

—— THE INFLUENCE OF MUSIC ON BEHAVIOR. Princeton, N.J.: Princeton University Press, 1926.

—— "The Development of an Experimental Psychology of Music." In Schullian, D. M. and Schoen, M. (Eds.), MUSIC AND MEDICINE. Pp. 367–386. New York: Henry Schuman, Inc., 1948.

—— and Fine, H. PSYCHOLOGY OF MUSIC. Pp. 19–44. College of Music, Cincinnati, Ohio, 1939.

Eagle, C. T., Jr. (Ed.) MUSIC THERAPY INDEX: Volume 1, 1976. Lawrence, Kans.: National Association for Music Therapy, Inc., 1976.

—— (Ed.) MUSIC PSYCHOLOGY INDEX: Volume 2, 1978. Denton, Tex.: Institute for Therapeutics Research, 1978.

Eby, J. "The Value of Music in a Psychiatric Institution." Pp. 31–35. OCCUP. THER. & REHABIL. (22), February, 1943.

Ehrenzweig, A. THE PSYCHOANALYSIS OF ARTISTIC VISION AND HEARING. New York: Julian Press, 1953.

Erikson, E. H. CHILDHOOD AND SOCIETY (2nd Ed.) New York: W. W. Norton, 1963.

Erikson, J. M. ACTIVITY, RECOVERY, GROWTH—The Communal Role of Planned Activities. New York: W. W. Norton, 1976.

Fischer, J. H. "What—And How—to Teach Teachers." N.Y. TIMES MAGAZINE SUPPLEMENT, September 9, 1962.

Fisher, S. H. "The Recovered Patient Returns to the Community." Pp. 463–473. MENTAL HYGIENE (42:4), October, 1958.

Gaston, E. T. "Nature and Principles of Music Therapy." MUSIC THERAPY 1954. Pp. 152–155. Lawrence, Kans.: National Association for Music Therapy, Inc., 1955.

—— "Man and Music." In Gaston, E. T. (Ed.), MUSIC IN THERAPY. P. 26. New York: The MacMillan Company, 1968.

Gilman, L. and Paperte, F. "Music as a Psychotherapeutic Agent." MUSIC AND YOUR EMOTIONS. New York: Liveright Publishing Corp., 1952.

Graham, R. "Suggested Procedures for Conducting Rhythm Activities on Wards of Chronic and Regressed Mental Patients." Unpublished Master's thesis, Univ. of Kansas, 1958.

Hanson, H. "Emotional Expression in Music." In Schullian, D. M. and Schoen, M. (Eds.), MUSIC AND MEDICINE. Pp. 244–265. New York: Henry Schuman, Inc., 1948.

Hevner, K. "The Affective Value of Pitch and Tempo in Music." Pp. 621–630. AMERICAN J. PSYCHOL. (49), October, 1937.

Highet, G. THE ART OF TEACHING. New York: Knopf, 1950.

Hollander, F. M. and Juhrs, P. D. "Orff-Schulwerk, an Effective Treatment Tool with Autistic Children." JOURNAL OF MUSIC THERAPY, vol. XI, no. 1. Pp. 1–12. Spring. 1974.

Howery, B. I. "Music Therapy for the Mentally Retarded," AN ANALYSIS, EVALUATION, AND SELECTION OF CLINICAL USES OF MUSIC IN THERAPY, E. T. Gaston and Erwin H. Schneider, Eds., The University of Kansas, Lawrence, Kansas: 1965. Pp. 135–184.

Hudson, W. C. "Music: A Physiologic Language." Pp. 137–140. JOURNAL OF MUSIC THERAPY, vol. X, no. 3, Fall, 1973.

Hughes, C. W. "Rhythm and Health." In Schullian, D. M. and Schoen, M. (Eds.), MUSIC AND MEDICINE. Pp. 158–189. New York: Henry Schuman, Inc., 1948.

Isham, A. C. "The Use of Song Parodies as Recreational Therapy for Mental Patients." Pp. 259–261. OCCUP. THERAPY & REHABIL. (24), 1945.

Jones, M. THE THERAPEUTIC COMMUNITY. New York: Basic Books, 1953.

Jorgenson, H. "The Use of a Contingent Music Activity to Modify Behaviors Which Interfere with Learning." JOURNAL OF MUSIC THERAPY, vol. XI, no. 1. Pp. 41–46. Spring, 1974.

Joynt, R. J. and Green, D. "Musicogenic Epilepsy." Pp. 501–504. JOURNAL OF THE AMERICAN MEDICAL ASSOCIATION (179), 1962.

Kirk, S. A. and McCarthy, J. J. "The Illinois Test of Psycholinguistic Abilities, and approach to differential diagnosis." AMERICAN JOURNAL OF MENTAL DEFICIENCY, 1961. Pp. 66, 399–412.

Klee, P. THE INWARD VISION. New York: Harry N. Abrams, Inc., 1958.

Knapp, P. H. "The Ear: Listening and Hearing." Pp. 672–689. J. AMER. PSYCHOANAL. (1), 1953.

Knight, Ludwig, Strazzula, Pope. "The Role of Varied Therapies in the Rehabilitation of the Retarded Child," AMERICAN JOURNAL OF MENTAL DEFICIENCY, 1957. Pp. 61, 508–515.

Kohut, H. "The Psychological Significance of Musical Activity." MUSIC THERAPY 1951. Pp. 151–157. Chicago, Ill.: National Association for Music Therapy Inc., 1952.

Kris, E. PSYCHOANALYTIC EXPLORATIONS IN ART. New York: International Universities Press, 1952.

La Master, R. J. "Music Therapy as a Tool for Treatment of Mental Patients in the Hospital." Pp. 110–114 in HOSP. MANAGEMENT (62), December, 1946. Pp. 110–114 in (63), January, 1947.

Lang, P. H. MUSIC IN WESTERN CIVILIZATION. Pp. 587–590. New York: W. W. Norton & Co., Inc., 1941.

Langer, S. K. FEELING AND FORM: A THEORY OF ART. London: Routledge and Kegan Paul, 1953.

Lathom, W. "Application of Kodaly Concepts in Music Therapy." JOURNAL OF MUSIC THERAPY, vol. XI, no. 1. Pp. 13–20. Spring, 1974.

Lee, R. E. "Music Therapy at Rockland State Helps to Resocialize Patients." BETTER TIMES (37:18), p. 3, January 27, 1956.

Luce, G. G. BIOLOGICAL RHYTHMS IN PSYCHIATRY AND MEDICINE. Public Health Service Monograph #2088. Chevy Chase, Md.: National Institute of Mental Health, 1970.

Ludwig, A. J. and Tyson, F. "A Song for Michael — The Use of Music Therapy as an Educational Modality within a Situation of Progressive Organic Deterioration." JOURNAL OF MUSIC THERAPY, vol. 6, no. 3. Pp. 82–86. Fall, 1969.

Marcuse, H. EROS AND CIVILIZATION. Boston: Beacon Press, 1955.

Meinecke, B. "Music and Medicine in Classical Antiquity." Pp. 47–95. In Schullian, D. M. and Schoen, M. (Eds.), MUSIC AND MEDICINE. New York: Henry Schuman, Inc., 1948.

Morrissey, J. R. "Death Anxiety in Children with a Fatal Illness," AMERICAN JOURNAL OF PSYCHOTHERAPY, 1964, 18. Pp. 606–615.

Mowrer, O. H. "Autism Theory of Speech Development and Some Clinical Applications," JOURNAL OF SPEECH AND HEARING, 1952, 17. Pp. 263–268.

Nadel, S. "The Origins of Music." Pp. 538–548. MUSICAL QUARTERLY, 16, July, 1930.

Nordoff, P. and Robbins, C. THERAPY IN MUSIC FOR HANDICAPPED CHILDREN. New York: St. Martin's Press, 1972.

Noy, P. "The Psychodynamic Meaning of Music—Part II." JOURNAL OF MUSIC THERAPY, vol. IV, no. 1, pp. 7–23, March, 1967.

Ponath, L. H. and Bitcon, C. H. "A Behavioral Analysis of Orff-Schulwerk." JOURNAL OF MUSIC THERAPY, vol. IX, no. 2. Pp. 56–63. Summer, 1972.

Pratt, C. C. MUSIC AND THE LANGUAGE OF EMOTION. Pp. 17 and 24. Library of Congress, Washington, D.C., 1952.

Racker, H. "Contribution to the Psychoanalysis of Music." Pp. 129–163. AM. IMAGO (8), 1951.

Radin, P. "Music and Medicine Among Primitive Peoples." Pp. 3–24. In Schullian, D. M. and Schoen, M. (Eds.), MUSIC AND MEDICINE. New York: Henry Schuman, Inc., 1948.

Reese, H. H. "The Relation of Music to Diseases of the Brain." In Podolsky, E. (Ed.), MUSIC THERAPY. Pp. 43–54. New York: Philosophical Library, 1953.

Revesz, G. INTRODUCTION TO THE PSYCHOLOGY OF MUSIC. Pp. 213–214. Univ. of Oklahoma Press, 1954.

Rimland, B. INFANTILE AUTISM: THE SYNDROME AND ITS IMPLICATIONS FOR A NEURAL THEORY OF BEHAVIOR. New York: Appleton-Century-Crofts, 1964.

Robinault, I. P. "The Scope of Music Therapy." P. 5. AMER. J. OCCUP. THERAPY (3), Sept.–Oct., 1949.

Ruesch, J. and Kees, W. NONVERBAL COMMUNICATION. Berkeley: Univ. of California Press, 1956.

Schneider, M. "Primitive Music." Pp. 4–16. In Wellesz, E. (Ed.), THE NEW OXFORD HISTORY OF MUSIC, vol. I. London: Oxford University Press, 1957.

Sears, W. W. "Processes in Music Therapy." In Gaston, E. T. (Ed.), MUSIC IN THERAPY. Pp. 30–44. New York: The MacMillan Co., 1968.

Seashore, C. E. "The Present Status of Research in the Psychology of Music at the University of Iowa." UNIV. IOWA STUD., vol. 2, no. 4, 1928.

—— PSYCHOLOGY OF MUSIC. New York: McGraw-Hill Book Co., Inc., 1938.

Seeger, R. C. AMERICAN FOLK SONGS FOR CHILDREN, Doubleday and Company, Inc., Garden City, New York, 1948.

Shatin, L. et al. "Music Therapy for Schizophrenics." JOURNAL OF REHABILITATION. Pp. 30–31. September–October, 1961.

Sherwin, A. C. "A Consideration of the Therapeutic Use of Music in Psychiatric Illness." THE JOURNAL OF NERVOUS AND MENTAL DISEASE, vol. 127, no. 1. Pp. 84–90. July, 1958.

Sigerist, H. CIVILIZATION AND DISEASE. Pp. 131–147. Ithaca, N.Y.: Cornell University Press, 1944.

Simon, W. "The Value of Music in the Resocialization and Rehabilitation of the Mentally Ill." Pp. 498–500. MIL. SURG. (97), December, 1945.

Simon, B., Holzberger, J. D., Allessi, S. L. and Garrity, D. A. "The Recognition and Acceptance of Mood in Music by Psychotic Patients." Pp. 66–78. J. NERV. & MENT. DIS. (114), July, 1951.

Slavson, S. R. A TEXTBOOK IN ANALYTIC GROUP PSYCHOTHERAPY. New York: International Universities Press, 1964.

Stein, J. and Euper, J. A. "Advances in Music Therapy." CURRENT PSYCHIATRIC THERAPIES: 1974, pp. 107–1 3.

Stone, A. A. and Stone, S. S. (Eds.) THE ABNORMAL PERSONALITY THROUGH LITERATURE. Englewood Cliffs, N.J.: Prentice-Hall, Inc. 1966.

Tyson, F. "The Development of an Out-Patient Music Therapy Referral Service." MUSIC THERAPY 1958. Pp. 129–134. Lawrence, Kans.: National Association for Music Therapy, Inc., 1959.

—— "Therapeutic Elements in Out-Patient Music Therapy." Pp. 315–327. THE PSYCHIATRIC QUARTERLY, Utica, N.Y.: State Hospitals Press, April, 1965.

—— "Music Therapy Practice in the Community — Three Case Histories." THE PSYCHIATRIC QUARTERLY SUPPLEMENT, Part I. Pp. 45–64. Utica, N.Y.: State Hospitals Press, 1966.

—— "The Community Music Therapy Center." In Gaston, E. T. (Ed.) MUSIC IN THERAPY. Pp. 382–388. New York: The MacMillan Co., 1968.

—— "Guidelines Toward the Organization of Clinical Music Therapy Programs in the Community." Pp. 113–124. JOURNAL OF MUSIC THERAPY, vol. X, no. 3. Fall, 1973.

—— "Child At The Gate: Individual Music Therapy with a Schizophrenic Woman." ART PSYCHOTHERAPY, vol. 6, pp. 77–83. Pergamon Press Ltd., 1979.

Van de Wall, W. "A Systematic Music Program for Mental Hospitals." Pp. 279–291. AM. J. PSYCHIAT. (6), October, 1926.

—— MUSIC IN HOSPITALS. New York: Russell Sage Foundation, 1946.

—— "Music in Hospitals." In Schullian, D. M. and Schoen, M. (Eds.), MUSIC AND MEDICINE. Pp. 293–321. New York: Henry Schuman, Inc. 1948.

Von Lange, I. DAS WESEN DER KUNST. Berlin, 1901. In Noy, P., op. cit., p. 14.

Williams, R. H. PSYCHIATRIC REHABILITATION IN THE HOSPITALS. Public Health Service Reprint No. 3223, vol. 58, no. 11, November, 1953.

Wood, M. M., Graham, R. M. et al. DEVELOPMENTAL MUSIC THERAPY. Athens, Ga.: The Rutland Center and University of Georgia, 1974.

Zwerling, I. "The Creative Arts Therapies as 'Real Therapies.'" HOSPITAL AND COMMUNITY PSYCHIATRY, vol. 30, no. 12. Pp. 841–844. December, 1979.

Subject Index

Author Index